Russian Empire
Poland
ngary
Mongolia
Ottoman Empire
Egypt
Persia
Tibet
China
Sudan
Arabia
India
Bengal
PACIFIC OCEAN
Siam
Philippines
INDIAN OCEAN
Borneo
Sumatra
Mozambique
Madagascar
Java
Australia
New Zealand
18
32
(53)
19
20
27
21
(52)
33
39
37
38
40
31
48
25
26
41
42
Battles
(49) Quebec (1759)
(50) Portobello (1739)
(51) Quiberon Bay (1759)
(52) Plassey (1757)
(53) Arcot (1751)

First published 1972
Macdonald & Co (Publishers) Limited
St Giles House, 49/50 Poland Street
London W1A 2LG

© 1972 Macdonald & Co
(Publishers) Limited

Printed in England by
Hazell Watson & Viney Ltd
Aylesbury, Bucks

Edited by Bridget Hadaway
and Sue Jacquemier
Cover designed by Robert Jackson

SBN 356 04130 1
Library of Congress Catalog Card
No. 76-172431

Cover: *(TL)* 18th century pistol.
(TC) The James's Square Macaroni, a print by Darley of about 1770.
(TR) The 4th Earl of Traquair, whose home was a major Jacobite centre in Scotland in the early part of the 18th century.
(LC) A soldier of the Lancashire militia on camp-watch duty: one of the troops fighting in Canada.
(BL) The Methodist Chapel near John Wesley's house; built about 1777.
(BR) Hampton Court, which was extended in the reign of William and Mary.

Title page (opposite): *(TL)* The "mitre" cap of the soldiers of the Royal Regiment of Ireland.
(TR) Toulon, one of the great French ports and arsenals.
(BL) George Washington as a young Virginian militia colonel.
(BC) A watch made by Thomas Tompion.
(BR) Queen Caroline, wife of George II.

We wish to thank the following individuals and organisations for their assistance and for making available material in their collections.

Key to picture positions:
(T) top *(C)* centre
(L) left *(B)* bottom *(R)* right
and combinations; for example,
(TC) top centre

Aerofilms *page 11(TR)*
Agricultural Economics Research Institute, Oxford *page 71(TR)*
Anne S.K. Brown Military Collection, Brown University Library *page 37(B)*
Ashmolean Museum, Oxford *page 53*
Batchelor, John *cover (TL)*, *page 44*
Brooke's Club *page 22*
Chichester Rural District Council *page 65(TL)*
Coates, Gordon *page 64(TR)*
Colonial Williamsburg, Williamsburg, Virginia *page 15(TR)(B)*
Cooper, A. C. *cover (BL)*, *title page (BC)*, *pages 22, 32(L), 36(C)(R), 41(TL)(TR), 47, 57(TL), 77(BL)(BR), 80(TL)(BL), 83(BL)*
Drury, G. *pages 13(TL)(B), 33(C), 35(T)*
Fleming, R. B. *pages 68(B), 75(BL)(BR)*
Gooders, Su *cover (TC)*, *pages 21(B), 46, 59, 63(L)*
Gooders, Su: The Bung Hole, Holborn *pages 56, 68(T)*
The Governor and Company of the Bank of England *page 21(TL)*
Greater London Council Library *page 59*
Guildhall Library *pages 21(B), 46*
Guildhall Museum *title page (BC)*, *pages 63(L), 80(T)(B)*
Haldane, Brodrick *cover (TR)*
Henry Ford Museum, Deaborn, Michigan *page 85(BL)*

H.M. Queen Elizabeth II, by gracious permission of *cover (BR)*, *pages 35(B), 79(B), 84(R)*
Historical Society of Pennsylvania *page 31(B)*
Hoddle, Karin *pages 43(BL)(BR), 62, 67(TR)*
Hulton Picture Library *title page (TR)(BL)*, *pages 7(B), 10(L)(R), 23(T)(B), 32(R), 39(BR), 42(L), 45(R), 49(TL)(B), 50(L), 51(BR), 52, 58, 60(L), 61(C), 69(T), 70(R), 72(R), 73(B), 75(T), 78, 79(T), 81(T), 83(T)(C)(BR), 85(TL)*
Leicester Museum and Art Gallery *page 71(B)*
Mansell Collection *pages 6(L), 7(TR), 8, 11(TL), 16(L), 24(L)(R), 25(BR), 36(L), 37(T), 42(R), 43(TR), 48(L), 49(TR), 50(R), 51(TR), 57(BR), 61(T), 76(T), 77(T), 77(T), 81(BL), 84(L), 85(TR)(BR)*
Mary Evans Picture Library *page 48(R)*
Marlborough, His Grace the Duke of *pages 11(B), 12(L), 13(TL)(B)*
Maryland Historical Society *page 31(T)*
Methodist Archives *cover (BL)*
Monitor *page 65(TR)*
Moller, Jill *cover (TC)*
Museum of English Rural Life, University of Reading *page 72(L), 73(TL)*
National Army Museum *title page (TL)*, *9, 13(TR), 40*
National Gallery of Canada, Ottawa *pages 2, 41(BL)*
National Gallery, London *pages 55(T)(B), 67(B)*
National Maritime Museum, Greenwich *pages 32(L), 33(T), 45(L)*
National Monuments Record *page 64(B), 65(C)*
National Museum of Antiquities, Scotland *page 7(TL)*
National Museum of Wales *page 61(B)*
National Portrait Gallery, London *title*

page (BR), *pages 6(R), 17(T), 18, 26(L), 39(BL), 43(TL), 81(BR)*
National Portrait Gallery, Scotland *page 19(L)*
New York Historical Society *page 15(TL)*
Palais de Versailles *page 33(B)*
Quebec House, National Trust *cover (CL)*, *pages 36(C)(R), 41(TL)(TR)*
Ridley, Christopher *page 20*
The Royal Exchange: by courtesy of the Gresham Committee *page 20*
Science Museum, London *pages 26(R), 80(R)*
Scott, Tom *pages 6(R), 19(L)(TR)(BR)*
Sir John Soane's Museum *page 68(B)*
Smith, Edwin *page 64(TL)*
Speaker, Rt Hon Mr, House of Commons *page 47*
Stewart, Peter Maxwell: Traquair House *cover (TR)*, *pages 19(TR)(BR), 34(L)*
Sun Alliance & London Insurance Group *page 21(TR)*
Syndics of the Fitzwilliam Museum, Cambridge *page 66(L)*
Taylor, M.R. *page 5*
Thames and Hudson *pages 57(BL)(TR), 65(B), 82*
Thomas Coram Foundation *pages 57(TL), 77(BL)(BR), 83(BL)*
Transglobe *page 66(R)*
Trewint Wesley Cottage Trust *page 51(TL)*
Trustees of the British Museum *pages 17(B), 33(C), 35(T), 41(BR), 75(BL)(BR)*
Trustees of the London Museum *pages 27(B), 69(B), 76(B)*
Ulster Museum, Belfast *page 5*
University Library, Cambridge *pages 70(L), 73(TR), 74(L)(R)*
Victoria and Albert Museum *pages 25(T)(BL), 27(T), 43(BL)(BR), 54(R)(C)(L), 62, 66(TR)(TL)*
Walker Art Gallery *pages 60(R), 71(TL)*
Wills Collection, Bristol *page 30(R)*

Macdonald
Educational

R J Unstead

Emerging
Empire

A Pictorial History
1689-1763

Volume Five

An overseas empire troubled very few heads when this period opened. James II had begun to tighten royal control of the American colonies, but he had been ousted and, during the long struggle with France in the reigns of William III and Anne, colonies were left largely to their own devices.

The triumphs of Anne's twelve years were followed by Walpole's peace, when the nation recovered its poise, amassed riches and let sleeping dogs lie quiet. This was perhaps a humdrum era of stocks and shares, building and manufacture, but it gave the country an underlying strength to meet the next challenge. When war started again, Pitt was able to call upon resources in men, ships and money that brought Britain the greatest victories and the most triumphant peace-treaty in her history.

By 1763, through chance, trade, and the fortunes of war, an empire had emerged which was larger and more widely-scattered than any of the empires of France, Holland, Portugal and Spain. But, in reaching this peak, Britain had won no friends and the greatest part of her empire was already restive.

R J Unstead

Emerging Empire

A Pictorial History
1689-1763

On the opposite page is General Wolfe at Quebec. There he lies, on the point of death, knowing he has achieved the impossible victory, that his men will take the city and safeguard an empire.

Quebec was only one in a catalogue of victories, for this was an era when British soldiers and sailors displayed the same kind of cocksure aggression as the merchants and industrialists at home. Men like Wolfe, Marlborough, Clive and Pitt had this flair for victory against odds, a feeling that sprang from a deep-seated confidence in themselves and in the men they led.

The same spirit permeated public life. The nation's self-confidence was expressed in the new steam-engines and workshops, in the great mansions and thriving farms, in journals, and songs like *Rule Britannia*. The 18th century Englishman, pugnacious, practical and insensitive, had yet to taste the bitterness of a major defeat.

Contents

The Settlement: Ireland

Jacobitism was born when the "Glorious Revolution" swept James II off the throne. The Jacobites supported King James and, for many years, their aim was to restore the house of Stuart. In England, they showed little readiness to take up arms and mostly contented themselves with keeping in touch with the exiled monarch. In Scotland and Ireland, however, the Jacobites were much more active, for division between Catholics and Protestants was deeper and feelings were far more bitter.

In 1688, Ireland, in particular, offered prospects of success. As Lord Lieutenant, Richard Talbot, earl of Tyrconnel, already held Ireland for James and, at the head of a Catholic army, he moved into Ulster to wipe out the Protestant communities which had declared for William and Mary. The situation contained one major snag. Whereas the Irish supported James because they wanted to recover their lands and free themselves from English domination, James himself had no desire to overturn the old order and regarded Ireland merely as a stepping-stone to the recovery of his throne.

Ireland during the Williamite campaign. The Protestants, mostly Scots and English, were settled mainly in Ulster. After the Battle of the Boyne (near Drogheda), Tyrconnel withdrew towards the Shannon, while Patrick Sarsfield led a heroic resistance at Limerick. Churchill, Earl of Marlborough, captured Cork and Kinsale in a lightning campaign.

James II in Ireland

In December 1688, James had fled to France but, three months later, he landed in Ireland, accompanied by a small force of French officers and agents. However, Louis XIV had failed to provide anything like the number of troops, money and supplies that were needed to make sure of success.

The Siege of Londonderry

Since the Protestants had taken refuge in Enniskillen and Londonderry, James's plan was to capture Londonderry, in order to deprive William of his chief port of entry. The task seemed easy, for Tyrconnel had some 40,000 men and the Protestants, crowded behind the city's crumbling walls, were not expected to resist for long. However, against assault and hunger, Londonderry held out until provision ships from England brought in the desperately-needed supplies. The siege lasted for 105 days and, after the men of Enniskillen had sallied out to win a victory at Newtown Butler, James's army retreated southwards.

Static warfare

William now sent Marshal Schomberg to Ulster with a poorly-equipped army, and while Schomberg was too old and cautious to achieve much, James was equally unwilling to attack, so the two armies did virtually nothing through the winter of 1689.

The Battle of the Boyne

The stalemate was broken when William himself arrived with a substantial army and James advanced to meet him. On July 11, 1690, the rival kings faced each other across the River Boyne, which William ordered his foreign regulars to cross in order to make a frontal attack. He also sent a force upstream to attack James's left flank and after some sharp fighting, the Irish retreated. James deserted his army to make for Dublin and then for Kinsale where he took ship to France. He never returned to Britain.

The last phase

With James gone and Dublin taken, the Irish still put up a stubborn resistance. Fighting continued for another year until the inland towns were captured and, in September 1691, Limerick itself surrendered on promise of favourable terms for Catholics.

That promise was shamefully broken. Since their religion could not be stamped out, laws were made to prevent Catholics from entering Parliament or attaining wealth and education. The country lapsed into poverty and hopeless resentment.

(Opposite): William lands on June 24, 1690 at Carrickfergus, which Marshal Schomberg had captured during the previous year. William's army included six Dutch, eight Danish and three Huguenot battalions of infantry. He moved south towards Dublin and fought James in the Battle of the Boyne.

The Settlement: Scotland

In Scotland, as in Ireland, the Revolution brought bloodshed and suffering. Religion had long been an issue of bitter strife, not merely between Scottish Catholics and Protestants, but between differing shades of Protestant belief. With Charles II's Restoration, the Church had returned to the rule of bishops (known as "Episcopacy") and, while bishops were accepted by some Scots, they were resented by the Presbyterians and detested by the extremists of the south-west, who held fast to the Covenant and regarded any other kind of religion as an insult to God.

In the Highlands, the Catholic faith was still alive and it was there that loyalty to the Stuarts went hand in hand with hatred of the Lowlanders. In this divided country, the news of William's arrival in England led to attacks on Catholics and Episcopalians, and it became clear that the Lowland Scots would accept William and Mary if the Presbyterian Church was restored to power. Not so the Highlanders. Under a leader who could unite the clans, they were ready to take up arms for the Jacobite cause.

A woodcut, depicting the death of "Bonnie Dundee". He was actually killed by a bullet.

The turbulent clansmen

The test of any Scottish leader lay in his ability to unite the clans. Even in the Highlands, the clansmen were constantly at enmity with one another, usually over cattle-raiding and jealousy between their fiercely independent chiefs.

Montrose, Claverhouse (known as "Bonnie Dundee") and, later, Bonnie Prince Charlie were three commanders who possessed such charm and courage that the clansmen would obey them.

Almost all the clans were united in their hatred of the land-grabbing Campbells, none more so than the Macdonalds. Their long-standing feud reached a tragic climax at Glencoe.

Scotland, showing the sites of the Jacobite victory at Killiecrankie and the Massacre of Glencoe. Blair Atholl was the marquis of Atholl's castle, held by him for King James.

Captain Robert Campbell who gave the order to butcher the Macdonalds. His niece was married to MacIan's son and he spent much time drinking and playing cards with the old chief.

The Massacre of Glencoe

Unrest in the Highlands caused William's government to demand an oath of loyalty from the chiefs. The oath had to be taken by New Year's Day 1692, and all had complied except MacIan, chief of the Macdonalds of Glencoe.

Delayed by snow, he swore the oath one week late, and this was enough for Sir John Dalrymple, adviser to King William. Having a grudge against the Macdonalds, he obtained royal permission to punish MacIan and, on February 1, a Captain Campbell arrived at Glencoe with 140 soldiers of the Campbell clan and asked for quarters.

For over a week, they lived amicably with their hosts until, at night, they suddenly rose and massacred the chief and 37 of his people. The rest escaped from the Glen, helped by a snowstorm and by the non-arrival of more soldiers who were to have sealed every escape route.

A penitential stool at which a "sinner" would have to kneel and publicly repent. The Presbyterian Church was extremely strict and intolerant.

THE Scotch Protestants Courage OR, The Destruction, Death, and Downfall OF DUNDEE.

To the Tune of, *Billy* and *Molly*.   Licensed according to Order

Heading of a song-sheet containing verses celebrating the death of Dundee—a triumph for the Covenanters, a disaster for the Jacobites.

"Bonnie Dundee"

Graham of Claverhouse, Viscount Dundee, had been notorious for his cruel suppression of Covenanters and, in 1689, he united the clans and raised a Jacobite army in the Highlands. General Mackay, sent to deal with him, had advanced through the gorge of Killiecrankie, when, from higher ground, Dundee's army appeared. Mackay's infantry fired one volley and were overwhelmed by the Highlanders' furious charge. In the moment of victory, Dundee fell dead and, with no-one of his quality to lead them, the clansmen were presently defeated at Dunkeld and their army drifted away.

The Union of 1707

It was a commercial disaster that brought about the Union of Scotland and England. Many Scots had settled in the English colonies of America but Scotland had no colony of its own, nor any company for overseas trade.

In 1695, the Darien Company was formed to establish a trading colony on the Isthmus of Darien (Panama) and attempts by English interests to suppress the scheme only made the Scots more enthusiastic to subscribe their money. Everything conspired to ruin the venture—climate, lack of provisions, absence of merchant vessels and Spanish hostility; the scheme collapsed in total failure.

Naturally, the Scots blamed the English in general and King William in particular but, after a period of ill-feeling when separation and even war were openly talked about, common sense asserted itself.

In 1707, the two parliaments agreed that the countries should be united. The Union was not popular at first, but it brought great benefits to both sides and, when the Jacobites took up arms in 1715 and 1745, the Union proved strong enough to bear the strain of rebellion.

The Articles of Union presented to Queen Anne. Scotland gave up her own parliament in return for full freedom to trade and compensation for Darien losses. A common coinage was introduced, and Scotland kept her own laws.

France the Enemy

A fact of life during this period was war—almost continuous war—between Britain and France. William came to England to oust James II because he needed English resources for his life-or-death struggle to save Holland from the grasp of Louis XIV. Having foiled French attempts to assist the Irish, William formed a grand alliance, called the League of Augsburg, against Louis, but this did not save him from having to fight at sea and in the Netherlands.

By dogged persistence, he fended off the forces of the enemy but, though he saved Holland, the position at the time of his death was even more menacing. The King of Spain had died childless, leaving his throne to Louis XIV's grandson; hence, it seemed as if France's power would become overwhelming, since, in close family alliance with Spain, she would dominate Europe and a vast overseas empire.

To counter this danger, Britain fought France in Queen Anne's reign, when the Duke of Marlborough's victories brought France close to disaster, so that, by the Treaty of Utrecht (1713), she could not upset the balance of power in Europe.

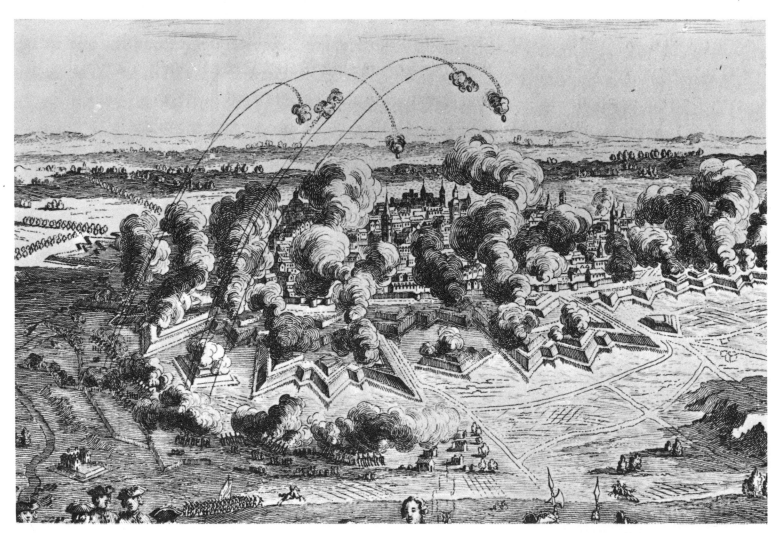

A contemporary print showing the siege of Tournai by Marlborough and Prince Eugene in 1709. Notice how the town is protected by extensive earthworks with pointed bastions, though these are no defence against mortars (short-barrelled siege-guns) firing explosive iron balls high into the air.

Professional armies had become so costly to maintain that commanders were reluctant to risk them in battle! Elaborate manoeuvres took place, with armies invading enemy territory but occupying entrenched positions without fighting major battles.

Sieges were the main feature of this kind of warfare, especially in the Netherlands, where William III and Louis XIV's generals played this complicated game to perfection. Marlborough, however, believed that a general should defeat the enemy on the field of battle.

A Scottish grenadier of George I's reign. His cap, coloured lapels and cuffs denote his regiment; he carries a musket and a grenade-pouch.

Foot-soldiers now had more dependable weapons, for the matchlock, with its smouldering "match", went out in favour of the flintlock musket.

Pikemen disappeared when the bayonet was invented, and this meant greater firepower, since every soldier carried a musket. Early bayonets were the plug type, fixed *into* the barrel; this prevented firing, so from about 1714, the ring bayonet came in and this fitted *over* the barrel.

Armour was no longer worn, and, for the next 150 years, infantry fought with muskets and bayonets only. Grenadiers were crack troops who went ahead in attack, throwing grenades. Cavalry were now effective against infantry only when formations were broken.

War of the Spanish Succession

The war-aims of Britain and Holland were to recapture the Spanish Netherlands, seized by Louis XIV, and to drive his grandson, Philip V, from the throne of Spain. Fighting took place in the Netherlands, in central Europe, in Spain and at sea.

Marlborough commanded the Allied forces (much hampered by Dutch officials) and worked closely with Prince Eugene, the Austrians' commander. After driving the French from Holland in 1702, Marlborough won the great victory at Blenheim (1704). Victories at Ramillies, Oudenarde and Malplaquet (1709), with innumerable sieges, brought France to the verge of collapse, but the Allies quarrelled, Marlborough was dismissed and by the Treaty of Utrecht (1713), which ended the war, France fared none too badly.

A partial victory

At sea, Britain's superiority was a handicap to Louis; the Spanish treasure-fleet was sunk, Gibraltar and Minorca were captured and the French defeated off Malaga. Yet the war was only partially successful; Holland was weakened beyond recovery and Britain was accused of betraying her allies.

Queen Anne and the Churchills

The rise and fall of the Churchills illustrates that, in the highest circles, royal favour was still all-important. As a girl, Anne made a bosom-friend of the dazzling Sarah Jennings and when Sarah married John Churchill, their fortunes rose in the world. Under James II, Churchill became a general but, in 1688, he went over to the side of William of Orange. Not surprisingly William never trusted him and when Anne quarrelled with her sister Mary and withdrew from Court, the Churchills shared her retirement.

On becoming Queen, Anne lavished every favour on her friends, making Churchill Duke of Marlborough and Commander of the Allied armies, while Sarah so dominated the Court that people said she ruled the kingdom. Eventually, Sarah's temper proved too much even for the placid Anne and when she was finally dismissed, Marlborough's fall soon followed, and the great general was brought home in disgrace, ruined by his wife's tempestuous spirit.

Anne's husband, George of Denmark (above), whose stupidity was a by-word at Court.

A broad-sheet in praise of Queen Anne (right), a popular sovereign, though she rarely appeared in public and spent most of her time at Windsor Castle. At her accession, Anne, second daughter of James II, was 37, a stout, kindly woman, not very bright nor in good health, but determined to do her duty and to support the Protestant religion. Her close friendship with Sarah Churchill helped Marlborough in his career but she afterwards abandoned Sarah for Mrs Masham, a more soothing companion. In her private life, Anne grieved for the loss of her 17 children who all died at birth or in infancy.

The whole Life, Birth, Glorious Actions, and last Dying Words,

Of Queen ANNE;

Who died at Kensington on Sunday, August 1st, 1714.

THIS most Excellent Princess was Daughter of King *James* II. by the Lady *Anne Hyde* his Wife, whose Father, was the great *Edward* Earl of *Clarendon*. She was Born at St. *James's* on the 6th of *February*, 1664. and had for her Godmothers the young Lady *Mary* her Sister, the present Duchess of *Monmouth*, and Dr. *Sheldon*, Archbishop of *Canterbury* for her Godfather. In the Year 1669, she was, for her Health's sake, sent into *France*, and after her return into *England*, she did not only acquire a healthful Constitution of Body, but likewise those Accomplishments which are seldom found in a Person of such tender Years.

By the great care of her Royal Uncle K. *Charles* II. she was bred up and Educated in the Religion of the Church of *England*, together with the Lady *Mary* her Sister, Confirm'd therein by the Dean of the Royal Chapel at *Whitehall*, Dr. *Compton*, late Bishop of *London*, 1676. His Majesty King *Charles* II. likewise made it his care to marry her to a *Protestant* Prince, *George* Prince of *Denmark*, to whom she was marry'd on the 28th *July*, 1683, in the Royal Chapel of St. *James*, by the Lord Bishop of *London*; to whom she was the most endearing and best of Consorts; their Love was such to each other, that *Europe* could not parallel them.

Upon the Death of his late Majesty King *William*, *March* 8. 1701-2, this Excellent Lady was Proclaimed Queen of *England*, *Scotland*, *France* and *Ireland*, and had such Series of Success during her whole Reign, as is not to be parallel'd in any preceding Prince. Under her happy Auspices, repeated Victories at Sea and Land crouded in with new Acquisitions of Glory upon the *British* Arms, and nothing was scarce undertaken but what was happily accomplish'd, by the Prudence of Her Councils, and the Valour of her Troops, who became a Terror to all Nations, under the Command of the Duke of *Marlborough*, whom the Emperor of *Germany* made a Prince of the Empire, for his great Services done to him, in retrieving his Country out of the Hands of the *French* and *Bavarian* Troops, by entirely Defeating those Forces. The Work of Ages was brought to pass in a 10 years War, and we had the Honour to be govern'd by a Monarch who was the Delight of her Friends and Allies, and the Terror of her Enemies.

At last, when she had effected an Union between *England* and *Scotland*, in vain attempted by her Predecessors; when she had reduced *France* to Terms of Peace, and made *Spain* submit to Conditions that enlarg'd her Empire; when she had done all that was Glorious on Earth, and stood ready prepar'd for a blessed Immortality in the Regions above, Death, whose Attacks she had hitherto withstood, with firmness of Mind peculiar to herself, laid his Icy Hands upon her, and seiz'd the Pledge of all our Vows and Prayers, by the means of an unexpected Distemper that had carry'd off her Uncle K. *Charles* the Second. Her Majesty had been ailing some

time with her usual Distemper the Gout, and being only on *Friday* last with Mrs. *Cooper*, one of her Bed-Chamber Women, was suddenly taken with a swimming in her Head, which struck her Speechless: Whereupon the Court was alarm'd, and no assistance was wanting to restore her to her Sences, and both a Cabinet Council and a Consult of Physicians was held thereupon; the first giving their consent, that the last should apply such Remedies as were thought proper in her Majesty's Case; which had such an effect, as to lull the whole Court into hopes of her Recovery: when, after they had to all appearance got the Mastery of her Distemper, by applying Blisters to her Head, the Apoplectick Fit return'd upon her, and after a little respite from the Agonies of death, wherein she behav'd herself with an entire Resignation to the Will of her Creator, she gave up her Soul into the Hands of God, on *Sunday* the 1st of *August*, 1714, in the 50th Year of her Age, and the 13th of her Reign, amidst the cries of a disconsolate Court and Nation, to whom she was an affectionate Mistress, and a truly beneficient Sovereign; who being ask'd on her Death-bed (by the Dutchess of *Somerset*) how she found herself; reply'd, *Never worse, I am going; but my hearty Prayers are for the Prosperity of this poor Nation*: and at the same time the Tears trickled down her Cheeks.

Upon which the Council (the same Afternoon) gave orders for proclaiming *George* Elector of *Brunswick-Lunenburgh*, and he was accordingly proclaim'd King of *Great Britain*, &c.

Her Majesty during her Cohabitation with Prince *George* of *Denmark*, was 17 times Quick with Child, and brought into the World 6 Children.

Price One Penny.

Printed by R. *Newcomb* in Fleetstreet.

The note which Marlborough scribbled after Blenheim and handed to an officer to deliver to Sarah in England. He asks her to tell the Queen "her Army has had a Glorious Victory. Monsieur Tallard and two other Generals are in my coach and I am following the rest". Despite her tantrums, Marlborough adored Sarah and she, for her part, never thought any man his equal.

Blenheim Palace, built in Marlborough's honour. Sarah spent years completing it and quarrelling with Vanburgh, the architect.

Sarah Churchill

Four years older than Anne, Sarah completely captivated the plain little princess with her beauty and sparkling wit. As Queen, Anne gave Sarah appointments which brought in a fine income but Sarah's domineering ways and flaming temper caused upsets, often tearfully patched up, which led to the final quarrel. Though she adored her husband, Sarah ruined his career and, after his death, her temper became more volcanic than ever and, known as "Her Graceless", she spent her old age making trouble and quarrelling with everyone.

Family portrait of the Churchills, with their children: John was an ancestor of Sir Winston Churchill.

Marlborough, the Great Captain

William of Orange's accession to the English throne brought England into Europe. In alliance with her former enemy Holland, she joined in the struggle against the ever-growing power of Louis XIV's France. By his own skill and courage, William saved Holland, but, towards the end of his life, a disaster seemed to have brought his achievement into ruins. With Louis' grandson on the throne of Spain and the resources of France and Spain united, it looked as if Holland and England, too, were doomed. William set to work to form a Grand Alliance against France and, after his death and in Queen Anne's reign, England produced a general who ranks with the greatest commanders of all time.

As Captain-General of the Allied armies for ten years, Marlborough won victories that changed the course of history; he broke the legend that the French armies were unbeatable and he forced Louis onto the defensive. If, at the Treaty of Utrecht, England betrayed her allies, that was none of Marlborough's doing, for, by then, he had been removed from his command.

Marlborough, the Captain-General. In an age that prized graceful manners, his patience and courteous charm to everyone were considered remarkable.

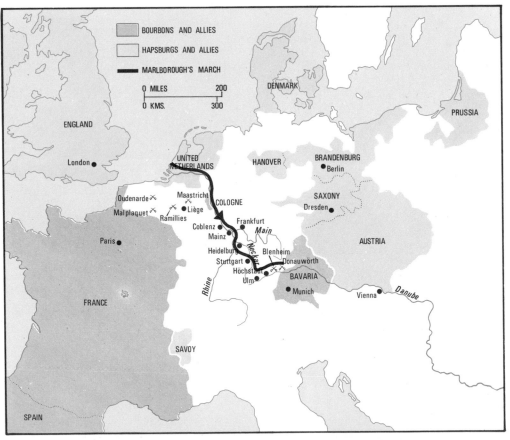

Marlborough's 400-mile march into Bavaria. His troops were unused to long marches, but he inspired them to make a supreme effort.

The Battle of Blenheim, 1704

When Louis XIV sent Marshal Tallard with a magnificent army to join the Bavarians and capture Vienna, Marlborough realised that if Austria were knocked out of the war, the whole of Louis' strength would be concentrated against Holland.

He therefore made the long march into Bavaria and joined forces with Prince Eugene, the Austrian commander. In a hard-fought battle at Blenheim, Marlborough's cool skill and Eugene's courage tipped the balance and, by nightfall, Tallard's army was broken.

Half his men were casualties and he himself was captured. This was Louis' first major defeat and the first resounding victory by an English general since Agincourt.

Marlborough at Blenheim, from one of the tapestries he had specially woven in Brussels to mark his victory.

Ramillies: after a terrific cavalry engagement, the British infantry advance to clinch a second victory.

The Captain-General

Although William III made little use of Marlborough's talents, he recognised his ability and, before his own death, ordered that he take command against Louis XIV. Queen Anne, of course, was delighted to honour the husband of her dearest friend, and Marlborough went to the Netherlands as Captain-General of the Allied armies.

He needed all his considerable qualities of tact and charm to manage the Dutch civilian leaders who constantly interfered with the army and never wanted their own troops moved away from Holland's borders.

In addition, Marlborough had to weld a collection of Dutch, German and British troops into an efficient force and, from the start, he showed them he was a fighting general, a plain man who shared their hardships and cared about their welfare. For their part, they gave him the devotion which only the greatest commanders can win from their men; they loved him and called him "Corporal John".

In 1704, Marlborough won one of the greatest victories in history. To save Vienna from certain capture, he marched his army at headlong speed across Germany, got between the city and the French and, joined by Prince Eugene, decisively defeated the enemy at **Blenheim.**

Having saved Austria, Marlborough next conquered Belgium by his victory at **Ramillies** (1706) and peace might have been secured but for differences between the Allies. In 1708, the great

Marlborough surveys the field before the battle of Oudenarde. He had marched his army, guns and baggage-wagons 50 miles in 65 hours and, with Eugene's support, completely defeated

Marshal Vendôme. By this time, the very name of "Malbrouck" filled the French with dismay, and peace might have been made if the Allies could have agreed among themselves.

general won the Battle of **Oudenarde,** captured Lille, and only the desperate courage of the French at **Malplaquet** (1709) saved Louis XIV's kingdom.

This bloody encounter was Marlborough's last. His enemies had won over the Queen, and the general who never lost a battle came home to face accusations of dishonesty. His opponents alleged he had accepted a commission of £60,000 on the army's bread supplies and had helped himself to a

quarter of a million pounds intended for foreign troops. Marlborough replied that the money had been properly spent on the secret service.

Whatever the truth, he was a masterly general of whom it was said: "If there had been no Marlborough, England would have sunk into a mere province of France, and the United States would have been French, not English."

A New World

England's American possessions in 1689 consisted of a number of separate (and jealous) colonies down the east coast, none of them stretching more than 100 miles inland. A population of some 200,000, including numbers of Scottish, Irish, Dutch, German and Huguenot settlers, inhabited a handful of seaports, some small towns, villages and isolated hamlets.

To the north and along the St Lawrence River lived a few thousand French settlers, wringing a meagre living from farming and trading with the Indians. The French also claimed the Great Lakes area and the Mississippi Valley, a vast territory known as Louisiana. Between these French areas and the English coastal bloc lay a wild no-man's land, inhabited by Indian tribes with whom the Europeans made treaties and traded for furs in exchange for knives, guns, blankets and alcohol.

From 1689, hostilities in Europe were reflected in America by almost continuous warfare between the English and French settlers. The English were more numerous and were increasing rapidly, but the French were far more successful in winning support from the warlike Indian tribes.

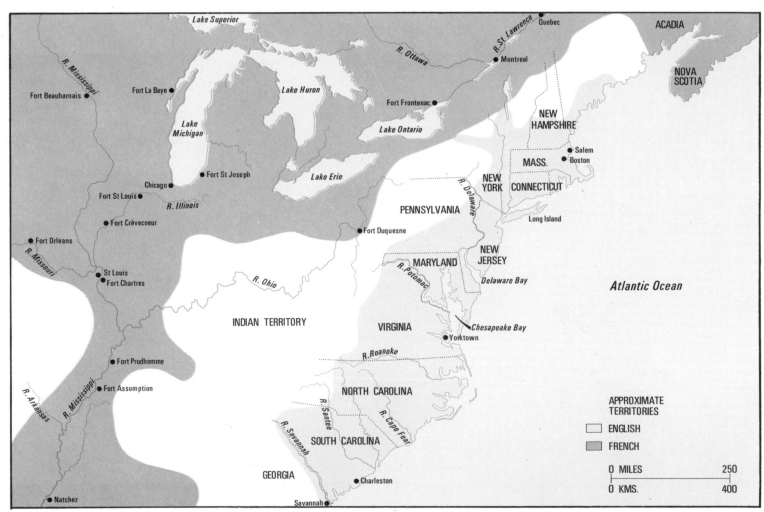

The French threat

France's Red Indian allies were a perpetual threat to the English colonists. War parties would swoop down upon outlying settlements, especially along the exposed borders of Virginia and New England, and every American boy had to learn to handle a gun, and to serve in the local militia.

By the 1750s, the French had pushed down the Ohio Valley and built Fort Duquesne, which was unsuccessfully attacked by young Colonel George Washington of Virginia. But the fort was eventually captured in 1758.

North America in about 1750, showing the areas of French and English influence. The English colonists felt that the French and their Indian allies were intent upon preventing them from expanding inland and a state of undeclared warfare existed all along the border. Fort Duquesne (later Pittsburgh) was the key to the coveted Ohio Valley.

Besides farming, trade and commerce flourished in the English colonies: here (holding printed sheet) is Benjamin Franklin in his successful Philadelphia printing-house.

Typical settlers in 18th century Pennsylvania: the farmer, probably a Quaker, is about to inspect his stock, while his wife teaches their son to read. Upright, God-fearing and industrious, the Philadelphia Quakers tried to live at peace with the Indians.

Founding a settlement

Colonists would usually look for a site on a navigable river, as at Charleston, above. They wanted a place which could be defended against Indians, which possessed fertile soil once the trees were felled and which could shelter sailing ships, since the market for their products and the source of their supplies lay in England, 3,000 miles away across the ocean.

Having chosen the site, the settlers had to build homes. Contrary to the popular legend, these were not at first log-cabins, except where German and Swedish settlers came, but wattle-and-daub thatched cottages. Soon, trees would be felled and the trunks split into boards for more permanent houses; the roofs were covered with wooden tiles called "shingles" and the heavy timber uprights would be set up by neighbours lending a helping hand. These "frame houses" were the typical colonial dwellings, though in the picture above, the buildings appear to be made of brick or stone.

Most settlers came to farm and even those who took to business usually possessed a cow and a vegetable garden.

An 18th century painting of the neat and prosperous waterfront of Charles Town (later Charleston) in South Carolina, founded by the English in about 1670 and named after Charles II. This was the first settlement in the new colony, whose early inhabitants included Englishmen, Scottish and Irish Presbyterians, Dutch and Germans, Huguenots and a few Quakers.

Principal crops were Indian corn or maize, wheat (especially in Pennsylvania), tobacco in Virginia and Maryland, and rice in the Carolinas. Cattle and pigs (called hogs) were far more numerous than sheep.

15

The House of Hanover

A German prince ascended the English throne in 1714 because a good part of the nation was determined not to accept a Roman Catholic king. After Mary, wife of William III, had died without children and Queen Anne's little son had died, Parliament passed an Act of Settlement whereby the crown should pass, not to James II's son, but to Sophia of Hanover. Sophia was the daughter of Elizabeth (the "Winter Queen", daughter of James I) who, long ago in 1613, had married a German, the Elector Palatine. Sophia did not live to ascend the throne but she passed on her claim to her son.

When he arrived in England, George I was 54, a portly little martinet, not without common sense but quite devoid of charm and majesty. Since he spoke no English and much preferred Hanover to England, he took but a small part in the government of the kingdom, which fell largely into the hands of the group of ministers known as the Council or Cabinet. The power of Parliament increased and the King, though he still possessed far greater authority than today, was no longer the centre of government.

Obverse of a gold medal to commemorate the coronation of George I in October 1714. Britannia places the crown on his head.

George I brought with him the Hanoverian tradition of father hating his eldest son. This intense dislike possibly arose from the son's resentment at the treatment of his mother; in Hanover, the Elector kept several mistresses, yet, when his neglected wife had a love affair, he shut her up in a castle for life.

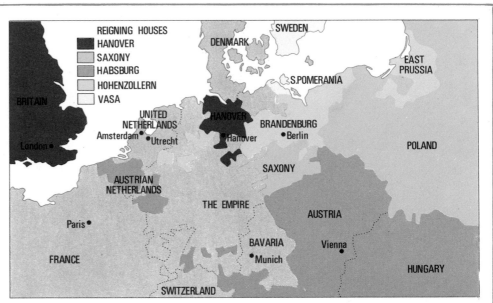

Map of Europe showing the position of Hanover. Situated on a plain, its lack of natural frontiers made the Elector concerned for its safety; George feared Sweden, was on bad terms with his son-in-law of Prussia and the Csar of Russia, and he very much wanted the two adjoining duchies taken by Denmark.

The beggarly Electorate

English politicians sometimes sneered at the Hanoverian kings' affection for their little duchy; they spoke as though it were wretchedly poor and a source of trouble and expense to Britain. George II never forgave Pitt for referring to his beloved homeland as the "beggarly Electorate".

In fact, Hanover was prosperous and well-managed, with a hard-working population and an efficient army which had fought for William III and Marlborough.

Certainly, George I used British warships and money to secure two duchies from Denmark to give him an outlet to the sea, and, during the next reign, Britain's foreign policy was much concerned with protecting Hanover from the French and even from Frederick the Great.

On the credit side, however, Britain gained opportunities for trade and better understanding of European affairs. Hanoverian troops stiffened the British army at home and abroad, and Hanoverian thrift improved the management of Court finances.

The first Prime Minister

The man who dominated English politics from 1721 to 1741 was a coarse jovial Norfolk squire who, though he never used the term, is regarded as the first Prime Minister.

Walpole had been Secretary at War in Marlborough's time, was a leading Whig and, luckily for him, was out of office when the South Sea Bubble burst—this was a share-buying mania which made fortunes for some (including Walpole) and ruined many others when the market collapsed.

Appointed First Lord of the Treasury, Walpole took speedy measures to calm the panic and clear up the mess. His success and George I's

Robert Walpole, the cunning squire who governed Britain for 20 years.

absence from Cabinet meetings made him master of the government and he used his power to carry out the policy he believed was best for the country. His aim was peace and prosperity at home and his motto, "let sleeping dogs lie", expressed his intention to steer clear of trouble and to avoid foreign complications, especially war.

Walpole had no scruples about keeping power by bribery, and he was adept at awarding pensions and jobs to his supporters. Walpole did much for the country, though he failed in two directions: he trained no-one to follow him, and he neglected to provide the arms and ships to defend the peace he had helped create.

Whigs and Tories

The two political parties of these times were given names that were originally terms of contempt. The Whigs were named after the "whiggamores" (rascally Scottish horse-drovers), while "tories" were Irish robbers.

In English politics, the Whigs were mostly townsmen—lawyers and business men—with a few great landowners and small farmers. They supported the Protestant religion, and included practically all the nonconformists or Dissenters. It was they who brought in William of Orange, though they supported parliament and checks on royal authority.

The Tories took the opposite line in everything. Most were country gentlemen and landowners; they believed in loyalty to the King and the Church of

A print of 1741, celebrating the failure of an attempt by the Opposition to persuade the King to dismiss Walpole. Leading his followers by the nose, Walpole watches as his enemies are run down.

England and this had put them in an embarassing position as regards James II.

Few politicians on either side were honest, for, as Walpole said, "every man has his price".

17

The "Fifteen"

In 1715, Jacobites in exile were agog with plans to restore James III, "the Old Pretender". Various factors seemed to favour their cause; George I was unpopular, riots had occurred in London and the west country, while, in Scotland, the Earl of Mar was openly preparing a rebellion. Abroad, Louis XIV still supported James and though the old King was short of money, he had hopes that Spain would provide a large sum for the Jacobite cause.

In their enthusiasm, the exiles seemed to forget that if the Stuarts stood a chance of regaining the throne, their supporters would have risen up in the previous year when George I came in unopposed. Moreover, James himself was the biggest stumbling-block to their hopes; glum and narrow-minded, he was not likely to inspire men to risk everything in his name, nor would he give the essential promise to protect English and Scottish churches. There was little in the way of arms, money or organisation to support a rebellion and, as though to underline its certain failure, Louis died, just six days before the standard was raised in Scotland.

The forlorn rebellion

When the Earl of Mar raised the Highlanders at Perth in 1715, English spies in France had already sent details of the Jacobite plans to London. Hence, the government was not taken by surprise and had strengthened the army and put a watch on the French ports.

Mar was no soldier. After some feeble attempts to take Edinburgh, he met Argyll and the Campbells at Sheriffmuir, a battle in which both sides showed more liking for running away than for fighting.

Late arrival

Highlanders could not be held together by this sort of leadership and Mar retreated to Perth, where the Pretender arrived in December. He was too late, and his dismal face did nothing to revive anyone's spirits. Barely a month later, he took ship back to France and Mar and some others soon followed him.

Meanwhile, a small body of English Jacobites had crossed the border to link up with some Lowlanders and a few clansmen sent by Mar. They moved into Lancashire but were easily dispersed by government forces and some 1,600 surrendered.

In the south, the Duke of Ormonde twice made landings in Devonshire but, finding no support, he too retired to France. Thus, by April 1716, all Jacobite activity had disappeared: the rising, doomed from the start, had not so much been crushed, as had simply petered out.

James Edward Stuart, "the Old Pretender", but rightful heir to the throne.

Winifred, Lady Nithsdale, who engineered her husband's escape.

Escape from the Tower

Lady Nithsdale went to bid farewell to her husband on the eve of his execution. She brought a weeping companion in a cloak, hiding some clothes. The companion left, another lady arrived and departed; Lady Nithsdale hurried in and out until the guards were thoroughly confused. Eventually, dressed as a woman, Lord Nithsdale slipped out of the Tower and escaped to France.

A Highland chief, one of those summoned to a hunting-party by the Earl of Mar. They met at Castletown in Braemar and raised the Scottish standard for James Edward.

What happened after the "Fifteen"?

The government, never seriously frightened, could afford to be merciful. Mar's abandoned Highlanders were rounded up and some 700 captured at Preston and in Scotland were sentenced to spend seven years on West Indian plantations.

Twenty-six officers were executed, two of the leaders escaped from Newgate Prison and only seven English and Scottish lords were brought to trial and sentenced to death. Four of these had their sentences reduced to imprisonment, two suffered death and Lord Nithsdale made a dramatic escape from the Tower on the day before his execution.

James Edward, finding himself no longer welcome in France, went to live in Rome. Here, the Pope gave him a residence and an annual income, and treated him and his wife as King and Queen of England. James remained in Rome when his son, Charles Edward, set out to win his kingdom, but after the failure of the "Forty-five", he became a mournful old invalid and died, almost forgotten, in 1766.

Maria Clementina Sobieski, the Polish princess, whom James Edward married. The emperor forbade their marriage, but a Jacobite, Charles Wogan, abducted her from semi-imprisonment and escorted her to Rome. Mother of "Bonnie Prince Charlie", her marriage was not happy and she died when only 32.

The World of Finance

The wars of the 18th century required vast sums of money, and the side which could find them was the likelier to win a long drawn-out struggle. Britain's ability to find that money was one of the keys to her success against an apparently more powerful enemy, and this came from new financial measures, a better understanding of mathematics, insurance, taxation and the balance of trade.

The English learnt much from the Dutch about banking and, in 1694, the Bank of England was founded. This was a most important institution, because the old methods of raising public money (by customs and excise duties and Land Tax) were no longer sufficient, and the Government had to borrow large sums from private persons and pay them interest every year. Thus arose the National Debt, which is the vast total loaned to the government. The Bank became the centre for these loans and it stood for the government's promise never to fail to pay the interest. It also became the most reliable place in the world to obtain money for business deals and ventures.

The founding of the Bank of England on July 27, 1694 by William Paterson and Michael Godfrey. The government borrowed over £1 million from persons who were formed into the banking company and received guaranteed interest.

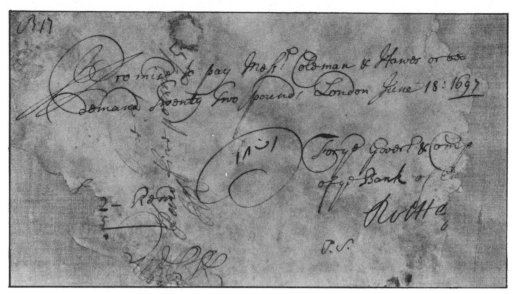

One of the early bank notes issued by the Bank of England, dated June 18, 1697. It is a promise to pay £22 on demand and, since the Bank could be trusted to honour its promise at any time, a bank-note was better than a bag of money. Business deals were easier and people did not have to risk carrying large sums in gold.

Firemark, no. 838, issued in 1711, to William Skelbon, who insured his house against fire with the Sun Fire Office. The sign on his wall entitled him to receive help from the company's private fire-engine!

An uncomplimentary picture of stockjobbers, the men who dealt in government stocks. The jobbers were accused of artificially raising prices to make profits for themselves.

The South Sea Bubble

A new development in London was the Stock Exchange, centred on two coffee houses. Anyone who held government bonds ("stocks") could sell them there to a private buyer. Shares in private companies could also be bought and sold at prices which rose and fell with profits and so on.

The South Sea Company, formed in 1711 to trade with Spanish colonies, was not doing well until its directors hit on a startling idea. They offered to take over the National Debt (all the money borrowed by the government), so those who held government stock would become shareholders in the Company.

The public thought this must mean wonderful trading prospects and rushed to buy shares which, in 1720, rose from £100 to £1,000 each. This share-buying mania led to the appearance of all kinds of fraudulent companies, until confidence suddenly stopped.

When people wanted to sell their shares and there were no buyers, the shares were useless. Panic set in, hundreds were ruined and accusations of fraud were hurled at ministers and officials. At this point, Walpole (who had made a fortune by selling before the crash) stepped in and restored calm.

Life in the Town

In the fashionable world of London and Bath, people enjoyed dancing, gambling and music. Above all, they loved company for its own sake, and would promenade on foot or in a sedan-chair to see each other and to be seen. A favourite way of spending an evening was to go to one of the many pleasure gardens, such as Ranelagh or Vauxhall, simply to walk about and "quizz" the crowds, to listen to music, and of course to refresh themselves on wine, punch or chocolate.

At the various Assembly Rooms, dancing took place from nine or ten at night until five next morning; and fancy-dress was so much the rage that, at one of the more brilliant assemblies, a dandy might change his costume three times in an evening. As at Bath, the gaming-table was the centrepiece, the magnet which drew men and women to risk whole fortunes on cards or dice.

The centre of London's night-life for less aristocratic folk was Covent Garden, where the Piazza and the side-streets were thick with taverns, coffee houses, vapour-bath houses, called *bagnios*, and other less respectable places.

The London clubs

The first clubs, with names like the October, the Mug-house and the Beefsteak, had no premises of their own; members met in taverns and coffee houses to spend a social evening together, with songs, toasts and conversation.

The aristocratic world soon formed its own version of these rather pleasant gatherings. A man called McCall opened a club in Pall Mall, calling it Almack's (an inversion of his own name), as a place where gentlemen of rank could meet their acquaintances, dine and play cards.

Other clubs were formed, such as White's, Boodle's and Watier's, but Almack's remained the most exclusive. An invitation card to Almack's was like a royal command. It was *the* place for gambling for high stakes—nobody could play without at least 50 guineas on the table.

There were numbers of less aristocratic clubs; Dr Johnson belonged to four—the Ivy Lane Club, the City Club, Sam's and the Literary Club, whose members included all the best known writers and artists of the day. The Blue Stocking Club held evening assemblies when ladies discussed literature and music.

A painting by Rowlandson of part of the Great Subscription Room at Brooks's, an exclusive club in St James's Street. Brooks, a wine merchant, took over Almack's and kept up its reputation for high-stakes gambling.

Genteel ladies

Among the gentry, parents usually chose husbands for their daughters, and a feature of the fashionable season in London, Bath and Tunbridge Wells was the "marriage market", when mothers did their utmost to arrange suitable matches. Questions of dowries and marriage settlements were haggled over like any commercial bargain.

For the young ladies, it was essential to be seen at their best at balls and assemblies, and on the whole round of entertainment, which was described as "tea, scandal, whist,

An elegant lady alights from a sedan-chair, a useful conveyance in crowded muddy streets. The chairmen carried it by two poles placed through slots at the side.

quadrille [a card game], dances, assemblies, raffles and masquerades."

At Bath, the ball was opened by the gentleman of highest rank leading out the most aristocratic lady, but, afterwards, the man of rank could dance with the merchant's daughter, and the lady with the penniless young officer.

The theatre was a regular pleasure, since a play seldom ran for more than a week, so there was a constant stream of new productions. Novel-reading came into fashion for educated ladies who delighted in the sentimental longwinded romances of the time. Travelling was another pastime for genteel folk who became fond of journeying about the country by coach.

Coffee houses

This was the era when coffee, brought in by the East India Company, became a popular drink. Men would meet for their "morning draught" and for longer evening sessions at their favourite coffee house. There they would find newspapers, pens, ink and writing-paper provided, they could collect their letters and leave messages for friends, but the real attractions were the company, the talk and the news.

Most houses had their special patrons: Whigs met at the Coffee House of St James's, Tories went to the Cocoa-Tree; writers gathered at Old Slaughter's or the Turk's Head, especially to listen to Dr Johnson, the great talker and literary man of the age.

Literary talk in a coffee house: a rather idealised picture of Dr Johnson holding forth to his biographer, Boswell. In the middle is Oliver Goldsmith, poet and dramatist.

At Lloyd's, in Lombard Street, merchants and sea-captains came to hear shipping news and to arrange insurance for their vessels and cargoes.

Life in the Country

The majority of Britain's population still lived in the country, for land was still the greatest producer of wealth. It was also the basis of prestige and position in the world. At the peak of society, the greatest aristocratic families owned huge estates which were tending to grow still larger. Immediately below the aristocracy came the landed gentry, who wielded considerable power in the counties and often controlled a parliamentary borough within their estates. Such men built themselves elegant country houses and collected fine libraries and pictures.

The country gentleman or squire also occupied a comfortable house, farmed part of his land and let out the rest to tenant farmers. It was he, living on the land, acting as Justice of the Peace, levying the rates and dispensing charity, who had the greatest influence on the lives of ordinary country folk. These included the tenant farmer, the independent yeoman and a whole range of workers, from skilled craftsmen to the poor labourer who eked out a miserable wage by keeping a cow or a few pigs on the common land.

A country-house kitchen: notice the variety of foods and the number of servants waiting on the gentry.

The country gentleman goes to church, passing the villagers, drawn up in a line to pay their respects to the landlord and patron. Here, he is Sir Roger de Coverley, the kindly, well-educated squire described by the essayist, Richard Steele.

Food and drink

All who could afford to do so ate enormous meals. Meat had pride of place, with all kinds of birds, from poultry and game, to swans and larks. Fish and oysters were popular; vegetables (except potatoes) were no longer despised and a great variety of tarts, jellies, nuts, fruit and cheeses, rounded off a meal. In polite society, beer, the national drink, was being ousted by gin, wines, port, tea and coffee.

Parson and squire

Parson Woodforde was an 18th century clergyman who for over 30 years lived in the same parish in Norfolk. He kept a diary, from which we know in detail how he and the people of the village lived. By most standards, he was very comfortably off, living in style with his niece and five servants; he entertained his friends to sumptuous dinners, travelled down to Somerset by coach, enjoyed the theatre at Norwich and gave a certain amount (but not too much) to the poor who, in hard winters, were usually near to starvation.

The Parson knew exactly where he stood in society. As an educated man of means, he belonged to the lesser gentry and stood much higher than the local farmers to whom, when they came to pay their tithes, he gave a fine supper— but in the kitchen.

For the Squire, a man of wealth, with connections at Court, who lived in a handsome mansion outside the village, Parson Woodforde had deep respect. When he was invited to the big house, he felt as pleased as if on a visit to royalty and, like everyone else, he looked on the Squire as the ruler of their little world. Fortunately for the village, Squire Custance was a benevolent autocrat who genuinely cared for his people.

The gentry hunted, fished and, with the introduction of shotguns, shot game birds for sport. Hawking and archery, therefore, went out of fashion. At home, gentlefolk played whist, dice, dominoes and the new game of billiards.

For ordinary people, the inn was the centre for news and excitement. Public coaches and hired carriages called there; the mail was delivered, and various amusements, such as cockfighting, bowls, skittles and shovel-board, would be organised by the landlord. A football match—a kind of free fight between the male population of rival villages—would take place at holiday times.

"Shovel-board" in an inn-yard, a pub game in which two players push or roll counters along the length of a raised board.

This great country house is Longleat, Wiltshire. Its gardens, orangery and parkland were laid out by Lancelot Brown, called "Capability" Brown, because he always said an estate had "capability of improvement".

Hunting scene by Wootton. Fox-holes were stopped, so that huntsmen could run the fox down in the open.

Country houses

Vast fortunes were amassed from land, trade and speculation (as in the East India Company and the South Sea Company), and dukes, financiers and merchants shared a passion for building mansions on their country estates. These palaces, designed by the fashionable architects of the day, were erected to display the owner's wealth and taste.

Built of stone, the outside was often faced with marble and adorned with classical columns and friezes, while the interior was furnished with the utmost luxury. Fireplaces, ceilings, library, wallpapers and furniture were specially designed and made for the house, regardless of expense —Walpole once spent £1,220 on a bed!

Gentlemen toured Italy to bring back ancient statues, busts and urns to add a touch of refinement to the salon or garden. Experts like Capability Brown landscaped the grounds, creating artificial lakes and waterfalls, and even servants' quarters and stables were designed on a magnificent scale to suit the great house.

Hunting

Like Walpole, who was said to have hunted five days a week, squires had a passion for hunting. Destruction of forests and increase in farming meant that herds of wild deer had almost died out, so gentlemen hunted the fox and the hare. They did not pay a subscription to join a Hunt, but kept their own packs of hounds and hunted across the open country, regardless of the owners. Hedges were now becoming more common, so the jumping quality of horses became important.

The Merchant Class

"The Commerce of England is an immense and almost incredible Thing", wrote Daniel Defoe; it was certainly in a flourishing condition and the driving force behind its prosperity was the merchant class.

Woollen cloth was still the country's foremost manufacture, accounting for nearly half its exports in 1700 and over a third in 1760. But the merchants did not confine themselves to woollens; they organised the weaving of silk and cotton, the production of coal, iron, pottery and glass, ship-building, brewing, transport, food and fuel.

The merchants of Bristol and Liverpool controlled the slave-trade and grew rich on the profits from tobacco, sugar and cotton. We hear of a Gateshead merchant, an ex-apprentice, who became the country's leading salt-producer and dealer in tallow; he owned coal-mines, imported tea, dyes, alum, flax and wines from all over the world and dealt in sugar, chocolate and tobacco. Men like him controlled the Bank of England, ran an empire in India, lent money to the government and influenced policies that decided on peace or war.

Robert Walpole, whose policy was to foster trade and cut down on government expenditure. He therefore did his utmost to keep Britain and pugnacious little George II from going to war. Although the Whig merchants supported Walpole, they would not have his Excise Bill.

The Custom House, London, 1714. Ships lying alongside the quay unload dutiable cargoes which, after duty is paid, are moved by cart and sledge.

Customs and excise

Much of the government's income came from customs and excise duties, customs being levied in imported goods and excise on goods produced in the country, such as malt, candles, soap and salt. Excise duties were unpopular because the excisemen could easily collect them, whereas smuggling enabled people to avoid paying customs on such goods as brandy, gin, tea and tobacco.

Walpole found the system in chaos and did much to reform it, issuing a new Book of Rates, reducing or abolishing duties on necessities and raw materials for industry. He also introduced the bonded warehouse system whereby tea, coffee and cocoanuts (for chocolate) were kept in special warehouses until required for sale; excise duty was then levied on them.

In 1733, he introduced an Excise Bill to add wine and tobacco to the list but so fierce was the opposition that he had to abandon the plan.

Smuggling

This amounted practically to a national industry and was very hard to suppress, because all classes supported it and few felt that it was very wrong. Ladies and gentlemen would drive in their carriages to meet the smugglers at an appointed place when a consignment of perhaps lace, brandy and tea was known to have been landed.

Parson Woodforde writes of "Smuggler Andrews" as though that was the man's regular occupation, and Admiral Vernon complained that in the coastal towns of Kent, hundreds of smugglers always kept weapons at the ready and, worse, passed on naval secrets to the French.

Smuggling was also an industry along the American coast where, in spite of British laws, New England merchants carried on regular trade with the Spaniards and the French.

An 18th century quay and customs house (left), where an officer levies duty on recently landed goods.

"The triangle of trade"

This was the famous (or infamous) trade route that brought riches to Bristol and Liverpool. Ships carried hardware and cotton goods to the coast of West Africa where these were exchanged for slaves provided by local dealers. Taken across the Atlantic to the West Indies, the slaves fetched good prices and enabled the captains to bring sugar, cotton and tobacco back to Bristol and Liverpool.

Colonies were supposed to exist for the benefit of the Mother Country, so their products had to be sent to Britain where merchants could sell them to other countries. In reverse, the colonies could only import goods from Britain.

Covent Garden, by this time London's main market for fruit and vegetables. The chief fish markets were Queenhithe and Fish Wharf until, from 1699, Billingsgate took the lead. Smithfield was a cattle market and not yet the centre for carcase meat, while the biggest general market was Cheapside, and its nearby streets like Bread Street, Milk Street and Wood Street which specialised in various commodities.

The Search for Trade

As the fortunes of Britain and France rose, the power of Spain and Portugal declined. Spain, so mighty in the 16th and 17th centuries, was now clinging anxiously to the remnants of power; her treasure from Central America had dwindled to a trickle that barely balanced her inability to produce the food and goods needed at home. The strain of perpetual war and defending her empire had proved too much for a country with an impoverished population, headed by a greedy aristocracy. Portugal, weakened by a long struggle with Spain, now possessed only one major

Rupert's Land

Newfoundland

New France

United Netherlands

Britain

France

New England

Azores Islands

Portugal

Spain

Louisiana

Tangier

Ceuta

Santa Barbara Is.

New Spain (Mexico)

Madeira

Canary Islands

Bermudas

Bahama Is.

Cuba

Hispaniola

Porto Rico

Jamaica

Cape Verde Is.

St Louis

Gambia

Ft. James

New Granada (Panama)

New Andalusia (Venezuela)

Trinidad

Guiana

Sierra Leone

Cape Coast Castle

St Andreas

Elmina

St Louis

Olinda

New Castile (Peru)

Angola

St Helena

New Estramadura (Chile)

Brazil

British colonies & trading posts
French colonies & trading posts
Dutch colonies & trading posts
Spanish colonies & trading posts
Portuguese colonies & trading posts

colony: Brazil.

Of the other colonial powers, Holland had prospered through commerce in Europe and the East Indies, though the cost of the wars against Louis XIV was to prevent further expansion. France had acquired enormous territories in America, besides trading interests in the Pacific and India, but, although the French colonies were tightly organised and well-run, the French never showed the same enthusiasm to settle overseas as the British.

Piracy

This period was the hey-day of pirates and buccaneers who, from the Caribbean to the Madagascar coast, robbed merchant ships and traded with colonies. Naval captains sent to deal with piracy sometimes took to the "trade" themselves and, in time of war, pirates became respectable, as they attacked Spanish forts and French shipping.

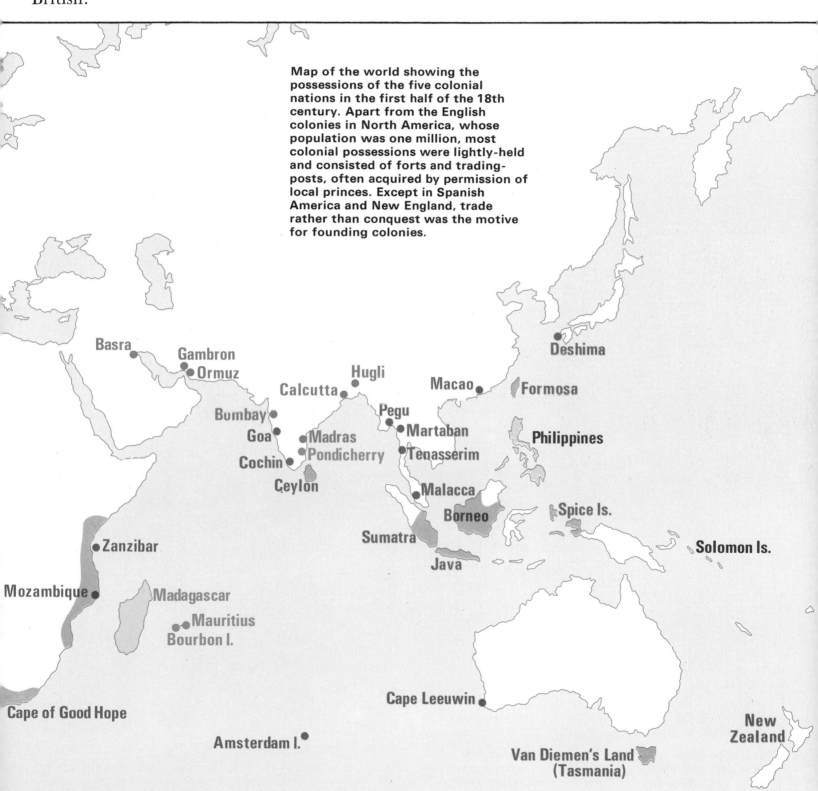

Map of the world showing the possessions of the five colonial nations in the first half of the 18th century. Apart from the English colonies in North America, whose population was one million, most colonial possessions were lightly-held and consisted of forts and trading-posts, often acquired by permission of local princes. Except in Spanish America and New England, trade rather than conquest was the motive for founding colonies.

America Grows

After the Treaty of Utrecht made Newfoundland a British possession, almost the whole of North America's eastern seaboard belonged to Britain (see p.14). Running south, there was Nova Scotia, the New England states (Massachusetts, Connecticut, Rhode Island, New Hampshire), New York and New Jersey, acquired from the Dutch, with Pennsylvania, and Delaware, inland. South of the old colony of Virginia lay the Carolinas and, lastly, Georgia, established in 1732, partly as a bastion against the Spaniards in Florida.

These colonies were developing in their own ways. Walpole interfered as little as possible and, while most were nominally governed by the King's Governor and Council, power really rested with elected assemblies. Steadily, they prospered from every kind of farming and from fishing, trapping and whaling; they exported vast quantities of rum and ships' masts and were beginning to make most of the manufactured goods they needed. Settled on the edge of a great continent, weeks away from Europe, the colonists were developing their own identity—they were becoming Americans.

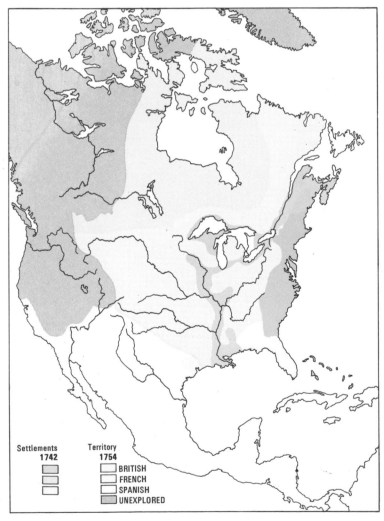

Areas of settlement in North America, 1742–54. The British colonies form a compact strip down the east coast, with all the advantages of good sea ports and straight-forward access to Europe. The population is now over a million. The French territory is too extensive to be held by a few settlers living mainly along the St Lawrence and around the Great Lakes. The Spanish in Florida, Mexico and California are intent, not on expansion, but on holding on to their possessions.

Settlements 1742 / Territory 1754
- BRITISH
- FRENCH
- SPANISH
- UNEXPLORED

A tobacco label of the late 18th century. From the early days of settlement, tobacco was the chief product to be exchanged for the manufactured articles the colonists wanted. It was grown chiefly in Virginia and Maryland, on big plantations worked by slave labour. The crop exhausted the soil in about seven years, which explains why the planters were greedy for land grants, since they constantly needed new fields.

Baltimore, Maryland, in 1752, when it had 25 houses and 200 inhabitants. As a centre for wheat and shipping, it grew rapidly in importance.

Philadelphia

Cities like Baltimore and Philadelphia flourished because of natural advantages like rich hinterland and fine anchorage. Philadelphia's Quakers became the leading businessmen, but the population included hardworking Dutch, Swedes, Presbyterian Scots, Huguenot craftsmen and German farmers who brought their crops into town in great wagons. Produce was exported to other colonies, to the West Indies and Europe. The city's schools offered a practical education and its college

The city and waterfront of Philadelphia (founded 1681) which, by 1750, was the most thriving port in America.

taught science and agriculture. This was already the second largest city in the whole empire.

War on Land and Sea

After Walpole's years of peace, Britain became involved in a series of wars at sea and on the Continent. The main enemy was France and when Britain recklessly embarked on the war of Jenkin's Ear with Spain, it was certain that France would support her ally.

An excuse for war lay in Austria. Charles VI, having no son, persuaded the powers to accept his daughter, Maria Theresa, as his successor. But, when he died in 1740, Frederick II ("the Great") of Prussia seized Silesia, one of Maria's richest provinces, at which France and Bavaria laid claim to other Austrian possessions and Spain also joined in. As Elector of Hanover, George II was deeply concerned and he decided to support Maria Theresa and this of course brought in Britain, with Holland and Savoy as allies.

Thus, the Continent became embroiled in a general war, in which poor Maria Theresa's interests were almost ignored. She fought indomitably but, when the war ended in 1748, she had not recovered Silesia. In any case this was no more than a truce: Britain and France were still at each other's throats.

Commodore George Anson, captain of the *Centurion* in which he sailed round the world. Given a small fleet, he set out in 1740 to "vex" the Spaniards, rounded the Horn, captured enemy galleons in the Pacific and reached home after nearly four years. His crews suffered terribly from scurvy, but Anson's example and seamanship had an inspiring effect upon his younger officers and on Navy morale.

War fever in the Commons: Captain Jenkins tries to show his severed ear to Walpole, while merchants clamour about their ruined trade.

The War of Jenkin's Ear

Spain's policy was to keep intruders out of her empire but, by the Treaty of Utrecht, the *asiento* gave Britain the right to sell 4,800 slaves a year to Spanish colonies and also to send out one shipload of merchandise.

English merchants used this clause to cover a good deal of illegal trading, yet they resented the Spaniards searching their ships. A Captain Jenkins roused public opinion by declaring that his ship had been boarded and one of his ears cut off in the ensuing fight. The country clamoured for war, much to Wal-pole's disgust, for he rightly feared that France would side with Spain.

The war began in 1739 with some naval successes by Admiral Vernon, including the capture of Portobello, but the Navy had been allowed to fall into a sorry state and further attacks on Spanish possessions in the West Indies resulted in failure. By this time, the war with Spain had merged into a greater struggle with France.

Anson's flagship in action against a Spanish warship. He captured it and brought home treasure worth £500,000.

The War of the Austrian Succession

The British fought the war in Germany, Scotland, the Netherlands and at sea. George II took the field with an army of British, Hanoverian and Hessian troops and rather luckily beat the French at **Dettingen** (1743), though he himself set a brave example, leading his men sword in hand and roaring, "Steady, my brave boys, steady!"

Little happened after this victory until, in the following year, England was in grave danger of invasion. The French assembled an army at Dunkirk and the troops had actually embarked when a storm shattered the transport fleet.

The French commander, Marshal Saxe, then moved into the Netherlands and, to save Tournai, the Duke of Cumberland (George II's son) brought up an allied army and attacked the French at **Fontenoy** (1745). The brunt of the battle fell on "the terrible English column" which fought gloriously but in vain, and victory lay with the French.

The scene then shifted to Scotland, where Bonnie Prince Charlie tried to win back the crown for the Stuarts, but he was finally crushed by Cumberland at **Culloden** (1746).

Meanwhile, with the Navy now in fighting trim, Britain had some successes at sea and the war on the Continent dragged on for two more years until it came to an inconclusive end in 1748. The struggle was merely postponed.

The battle of Dettingen, when George II commanded a mixed army (the British are on the left) and drove the French across the river Main.

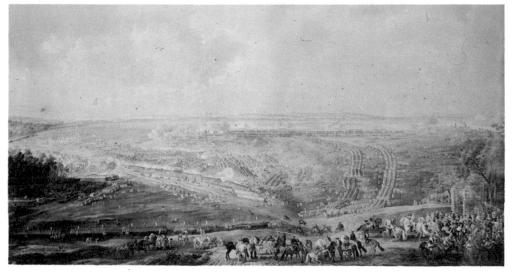

Fontenoy: the British (red blur, left) retreat in disorder under heavy French attacks from three sides.

The "Forty-Five"

In July 1745, Charles Edward landed on the west coast of Scotland with only seven companions. His supply ship had been lost, but his gallant air overcame the chieftains' doubts and they raised the clans and followed him to Edinburgh. An English force was easily defeated at Prestonpans but Charles Edward lingered in the capital, waiting for a general rising in his favour. It never came and the government won time to bring back Cumberland and the army from abroad.

It was November before Charles began the march to London with 5,000 Highlanders; he evaded General Wade's army and came down through Lancashire as far as Derby. But the English Jacobites never stirred and on "Black Friday", the chieftains decided to turn back. Beating off their pursuers, they reached Glasgow and retreated into the Highlands. Cumberland followed remorselessly and smashed their army at Culloden Moor. With a price on his head, Charles Edward wandered about for five months, protected by his heroic supporters, until a ship carried him to France. He left behind an immortal legend, but the Jacobite cause was finished.

"Bonnie Prince Charlie" (above), whose charm and bravery hardly made up for his poor strategy and judgment.

The story of the '45 (right): the map shows how Charles Edward came from France, landed on the west coast, crossed the Highlands to Edinburgh and marched into the heart of England.

During his retreat, he had successes in Scotland, but Cumberland took no chances and pressed on slowly with superior, well-disciplined troops until he overhauled the rebels at Culloden Moor. Flora MacDonald disguised Charles as a maid and enabled him to reach Skye and escape.

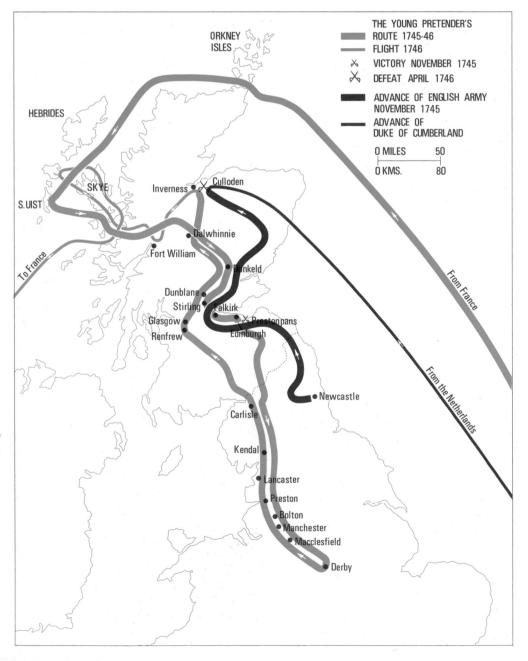

Defeat at Culloden Moor

Cumberland reached Aberdeen in February 1746 and waited there, building up his supplies from cruisers, which dispersed a French fleet bringing aid to Charles Edward.

In April, he advanced towards Inverness and found the Scots encamped on the open moor of Culloden, instead of in a stronger position advised by Lord George Murray. Murray's night attack on the enemy camp failed and, next day, Cumberland's army, 9,000 strong, attacked Charles Edward's 5,000 exhausted men.

The Highlanders had to endure artillery fire before they charged on the right with their usual fury, but were cut down by the regulars' disciplined fire; the left wing soon broke and Cumberland clinched his victory with cavalry charges.

Charles Edward escaped when two officers seized his bridle and forced him from the field. For three months, Cumberland patrolled the Highlands, hunting down the fugitives and burning their crofts, earning the name "the Butcher".

William, Duke of Cumberland (above), who commanded the government's army.

Hand-to-hand fighting at Culloden Moor, April 16, 1746 (below). The Highlanders lost 2,000 killed and captured to only 310 English killed and wounded.

War over the Colonies

From the time of the first settlements in America until the Treaty of Paris in 1763, the English settlers felt menaced by the Indians who occupied the vast interior and by the French, who held Canada and a great arc of land to the west. A clash was inevitable and it came over the Ohio Valley on which the French and Virginians cast covetous eyes. Both sides cultivated the Indians' friendship, as raids and skirmishes took place in the disputed territory.

From 1689, when the Mother Countries entered upon a long period of enmity, the French and English settlers became involved in their own struggle. They suffered savage cruelties and they looked to their home governments to help them out with regular troops.

In 1754, these sporadic hostilities developed into war, a war in which the French were generally successful up until 1758. In that year, the tide turned and, thanks to new commanders, the British prevailed. Quebec was captured and when peace was signed in 1763, France yielded almost all her American possessions to Britain.

An American rifleman of the early 18th century. All the colonies raised militia in which every able-bodied man had to serve—Massachusetts, for instance, called on every man between 16 and 60, and the penalty for dodging military service was death.

A French soldier outside the walls of Quebec. Under excellent officers like Montcalm and Bougainville, the French had repulsed two British attempts to capture Quebec before 1759.

An English redcoat in Canada. Armed with a "Brown Bess" musket, he wears a tricorne hat, white breeches and black gaiters. His hair had to be greased and heavily powdered.

The wrong way to fight a war

One reason for the disasters which the colonists suffered in the early stages of the war against the French and the Indians was their own lack of unity. Each colony followed its own course without regard to the others. The Philadelphia Quakers, for instance, refused to vote money for defence and New York persisted in trading guns to the Indians.

In addition, the militia, though good marksmen, were undisciplined and often at loggerheads with the British regulars, who looked on them as un-trained bumpkins. Hence, the force which Braddock led against Fort Duquesne in 1755 was in poor fighting trim. The militiamen had had too much rum to drink and the redcoats knew nothing about fighting in the backwoods. Forming squares and firing their muskets in volleys were the wrong tactics against an enemy operating behind trees and dense cover. The result was a disastrous defeat which encouraged the Indians to step up their attacks all along the frontier.

Unofficial war

Ill-feeling between the rival settlers came to a head in 1754, when a party of Virginians began to build a fort at the Forks, where two rivers became the Ohio River. This was a vital spot because whoever possessed a strong-point there could command the Ohio valley.

A French expeditionary force drove off the Virginians and built Fort Duquesne to dominate the region. The Virginians did not give up. Their militia, led by 22-year-old Colonel George Washington, advanced to capture the fort but were repulsed, and this setback caused the British government to send out General Braddock with two regiments of regular soldiers. The redcoats suffered a humiliating defeat, Braddock was killed and Washington narrowly escaped death.

Indian allies

War now flared up all along the frontier region, where Washington's small force of militiamen tried to protect the settlers from slaughter by Indian warriors urged on by their French allies.

Fortunately, the Iroquois tribes, known as the Six Nations, gave their support to the British. Thus, by 1756, when the Seven Years' War broke out in Europe, the American colonists had already been at war for two years.

A Chief and Medicine Man of the Mandan tribe in full ceremonial dress. After the French defeat, the Indians carried on the fight against the British settlers.

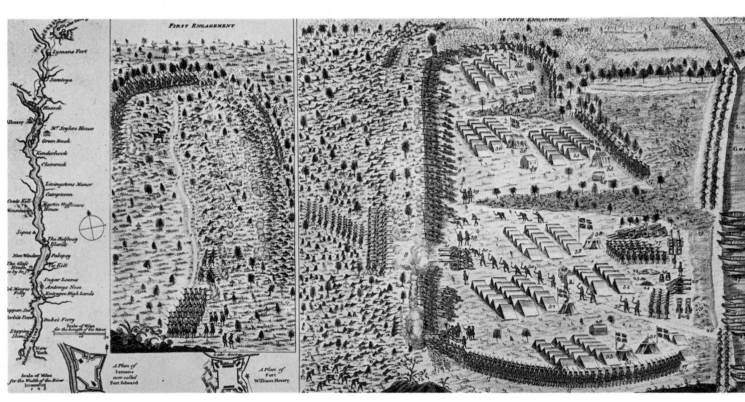

A pictorial map of the Battle of Lake George in 1755, drawn by an eye-witness. The British and their Mohawk allies are on the right, while the French and Indians attack from the left; on this occasion, they were defeated.

The French and Indian War

When, in 1756, after two years of unofficial fighting in America, a world war broke out between Britain and France, the colonists' position was a gloomy one. They had done badly so far and the commander now sent out from England, the Earl of Loudon, offended the colonists by his arrogance and disgusted them with his poor generalship.

The French, on the other hand, were led by the brilliant Marquis de Montcalm who soon captured Fort Oswego and Fort William Henry. Loudon was recalled, but his replacement, Major General Abercomby, was an even greater disaster. In an attack on Fort Ticonderoga, he failed to use his artillery before ordering the infantry to make a frontal assault, which was repulsed with heavy losses.

Ticonderoga, however, was the last of the French victories, for, in England, the great William Pitt had taken charge of the war and one of his first moves was to replace the inefficient commanders by younger and more capable men.

To America, he sent Lord Amherst and, as his second-in-command, General James Wolfe, an unorthodox soldier who had already seen a good deal of action. Between them, these new commanders drove the French from their strongpoints on Lake Ontario and in the Ohio Valley, captured the key port of Louisbourg and, in 1759, Wolfe won his immortal victory at Quebec.

The Seven Years' War

The Seven Years' War, 1756–63, was really a continuation of the Anglo-French struggle, with an exchange of partners. France now teamed up with Austria and Russia against Britain and Frederick the Great of Prussia. This latter combination suffered some heavy reverses, for France beat the British at sea, in North America and India, while Frederick was defeated almost beyond recovery and, to George II's agonised dismay, Cumberland lost Hanover.

These disasters brought William Pitt to the rescue. Declaring that he alone could save the country, he appointed new generals, despatched troops and gold to save Frederick and waged world war with such far-sighted skill that he made his boast good. The British Navy recovered the initiative and did much to ensure Wolfe's capture of Quebec and Clive's triumph in India; Frederick conjured victories against the odds and, in 1759, the "Year of Victories", a jubilant public heard nothing but good news. However, when George III came to the throne, the policy was peace, and Pitt left the scene. "The Great Commoner" had seen his country prevail.

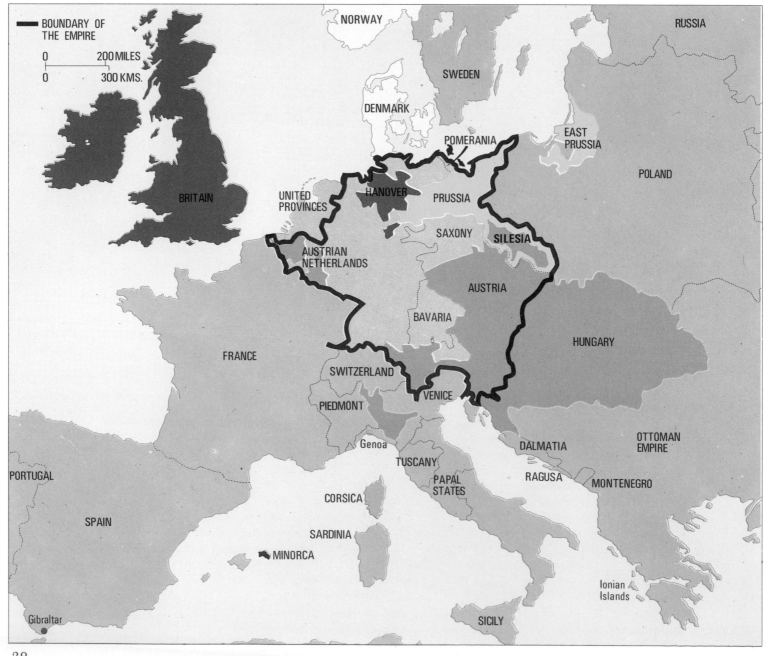

BOUNDARY OF THE EMPIRE

0 — 200 MILES
0 — 300 KMS.

NORWAY
RUSSIA
SWEDEN
DENMARK
POMERANIA
EAST PRUSSIA
POLAND
BRITAIN
UNITED PROVINCES
HANOVER
PRUSSIA
SAXONY
SILESIA
AUSTRIAN NETHERLANDS
AUSTRIA
BAVARIA
FRANCE
HUNGARY
SWITZERLAND
VENICE
PIEDMONT
Genoa
DALMATIA
OTTOMAN EMPIRE
TUSCANY
RAGUSA
MONTENEGRO
PORTUGAL
PAPAL STATES
CORSICA
SPAIN
SARDINIA
MINORCA
Ionian Islands
Gibraltar
SICILY

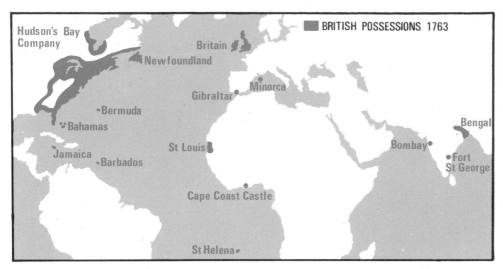

Map showing Britain's empire after the Treaty of Paris. Its chief possessions were in North America, the West Indies and India, with outposts linking these areas. Sea-power was obviously the means by which the empire was won and which held it together.

Outcome of the war

By the Treaty of Paris, France yielded Canada to Britain and all her possessions east of the Mississippi; in India, she lost everything, except five trading stations. Britain gained Canada, various West Indian islands, Senegal, Bengal, Minorca and (from Spain) Florida. She restored Cuba and the Philippines to Spain, Guadeloupe and Martinique to France. Prussia kept Silesia.

Though the treaty was a triumph for Britain, people felt that if Pitt had still been in office, the gains would have been greater.

In America, the colonists felt no gratitude for British protection and did not help pay for policing the new territories.

"The Great Commoner", William Pitt (later Earl of Chatham); George II hated him, but they came to terms.

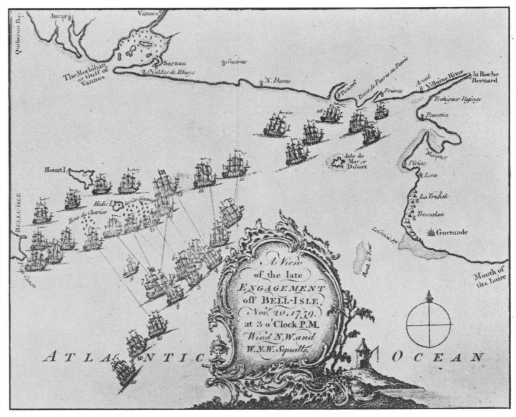

The Battle of Quiberon Bay, 1759. When a French fleet took refuge in rocky Quiberon Bay, Brittany, Admiral Hawke sailed boldly in and destroyed ten warships in a gale. After this, the French navy, scattered in various ports, could not face the British.

Europe's boundaries during the war (opposite). The Empire was now a loose partnership of German states, presided over by an Austrian Emperor of the Hapsburg family. Frederick the Great, fending off French, Austrian and Russian armies, fought with amazing tenacity and skill. Another brilliant general was Ferdinand of Brunswick, who replaced Cumberland, recovered Hanover and won the battle of Minden (1759).

Pitt's role in the war

This dynamic man was a patriot. He loved England passionately and his contempt for the corrupt behaviour of fellow-politicians made him popular in the country. He held power by his mastery of Parliament, quelling all opposition by force of tremendous oratory and often by a mere look.

By sheer personality, he imposed his will on the Cabinet, sending out fleets, choosing commanders as he pleased, planning campaigns and pouring out gold to sustain Frederick without regard to the War Office or Treasury. His policy was to hit France hard and often, using the Navy to attack her coasts and, above all, to prevent her sending reinforcements to America and India.

39

The Fall of Canada

It was the French who took the lead in exploring and settling eastern Canada. Quebec was founded as early as 1608, and New France came into being, a vast country, lightly-held but under unified control, with a warlike people who lived on close terms with the Indians. French explorers moved along the waterways, intent upon linking up their colony of Louisiana in the south with Canada in the north. If they did so, the English colonists would be shut in, unable to expand westwards.

At the outbreak of the Seven Years' War, the French held numerous forts and two major strongholds, Quebec and Louisbourg on Cap Breton Island, and they struck hard at the British, capturing Fort Oswego and Fort William Henry. Pitt saw that the key to the situation was Louisbourg and he laid plans to capture the fortress and to cut French communications between Ohio and Canada. Oswego and Fort Duquesne were captured and in 1758 Amherst and Admiral Boscawen took Louisbourg itself. British warships could now sail up the St Lawrence River and the scene was set for an assault on Quebec.

How Quebec was taken

At 32, General Wolfe was given command of the expedition to capture Quebec. Admiral Saunders safely conveyed the troops up the St Lawrence to where Quebec stood, high above the river, defended by 100 guns and an army under Montcalm, the brilliant French commander.

After a summer of intense effort, Wolfe was in despair, until he noticed a tiny path leading up the cliff. By night, he got a party ashore and they scaled the heights to overpower the sentinels and, at dawn, 4,500 men stood facing Quebec.

Montcalm's attack was shattered by two volleys from the British infantry,

September 13, 1759: British troops in position on the Plains of Abraham, overlooking Quebec, while reinforcements arrive by boat. Notice the fieldgun being hauled by sailors.

and his army fled in disorder. But Wolfe himself was killed, and Montcalm died of wounds a few days before Quebec surrendered.

A British sergeant of infantry (above): from 1700, sergeants carried a halberd.

Montcalm's death (right): he had been shot when rallying his troops.

Victory medal showing Britannia's head, laurel wreath, trident and standard, with the names of Wolfe and Admiral Saunders, whose seamanship played a vital role.

Detail from *The Death of Wolfe* (left) by Benjamin West: already wounded, he had dashed forward to order the charge, when he was shot in the chest. Dying, he still gave his final orders for the capture of Quebec.

After the capture of Quebec

Wolfe's immortal victory did not bring about the immediate fall of Canada. A position of great strategic importance had been captured, but it still had to be held and, with the onset of winter, the fleet had departed.

The French army, now under Lévis, had withdrawn towards Montreal, so the 7,300 British troops, commanded by Murray, were left in Quebec, knowing that they would come under attack in the spring.

During the terrible winter, frostbite and scurvy so reduced their numbers that they were sharply defeated when Lévis came up in April. However, they retired in good order into the city and, while the French were bringing up their guns, a warship appeared in the river. To their joy, it was British and when more warships arrived, Lévis decided to raise the siege.

General Amherst was now able to launch a three-fold attack on Montreal

—up the St Lawrence from Quebec, down the river from Lake Ontario and across Lake Champlain. His combined forces totalled 17,000 men, against whom Vaudreuil, the French commander, could barely muster 2,500, for the militia had gone home and the Indians and even some regulars had deserted.

On September 8, 1760, Vaudreuil surrendered and the whole of Canada passed into British hands.

The Race for India

The chief European rivals in India were the French and English trading companies, both of which held a number of stations or factories, leased from native rulers. As in America, the English seemed stronger but the French possessed some important advantages: in 1741, the governor of their headquarters at Pondicherry was Joseph Dupleix, a man of immense drive who had the support of excellent military and naval commanders. In India's chaotic condition, Dupleix found he could advance French interests by supporting one warring prince against another and he had well-nigh completed his plan to bring all southern India under French influence when the English woke up to their own danger.

At this point, Robert Clive restored British prestige by holding Arcot (1751) against a French-backed prince and putting the British candidate on his throne. Clive's next triumph was in Bengal where, again, he changed the situation by defeating a powerful nawab. The victory at Plassey (1757) brought Bengal under British rule and, three years later, French ambitions came to an end with the capture of Pondicherry.

Joseph Dupleix (1697–1763) who went to India as a young man and proved himself so capable that he became Governor-General of the French establishments. High-handed and quarrelsome, he was nevertheless unlucky to come up against so brilliant an opponent as Clive, and he received all too little support from his ungrateful government. Ordered home in disgrace in 1754, poor Dupleix died in poverty.

Trading-fort at Surat, where goods were assembled for export. Surat was the East India Company's H.Q. before Bombay.

How trade led to conquest

The English had been trading in India since 1601 and, for many years, their interests centred upon cotton goods, silks, spices, tea and saltpetre, for they had no intention of getting mixed up with political affairs.

The French came on the scene later—from 1664—though it was not until 1720 onwards that they began to rival the British. However, the decline of the Mogul Empire left India wide open to a take-over by any power with superior organisation, weapons and supporting fleets.

After Clive had destroyed French influence, the British found themselves ruling vast areas—Bengal and the districts around Bombay and Madras. Later wars and general anarchy made the British decide it would be simpler to rule India than to stand aside. Trade had produced some surprising results.

Clive of India, the family "black sheep" who founded an empire.

"The Heaven-born general"

A harum-scarum lad of 18, Robert Clive was sent to India as a clerk in the East India Company and, when the French captured Madras, he escaped and joined the Company's force as a junior officer.

A huge army was besieging Trichinopoly, the last English-held town, when Clive volunteered to draw off the enemy by capturing Arcot, their capital. With a tiny force, he did so and held the town's crumbling fortifications for 53 days against enormous odds. This feat and other successes restored British prestige and Clive came home a hero.

After he returned to India, Surajah Dowlah, who favoured the French, seized Calcutta and caused the deaths of 123 British people by imprisoning them in a tiny cell. To avenge the Black Hole of Calcutta, Clive came north to Bengal, defeated Dowlah and retook the trading-post. With only 3,000 troops against 60,000, he decided to overthrow the tyrant and, at Plassey (1757), aided by a secret pact with one of the Indian commanders, he won an overwhelming victory.

In the next three years, working with Colonel Eyre Coote and an efficient naval squadron, he destroyed all trace of the French influence in India.

As Governor of Bengal, Clive proved himself as brilliant an administrator as a general. But, in ruling firmly, he made enemies and came home to face those who accused him of corruption. Though he triumphed, depression set in and the man whom Pitt called "the Heaven-born general", took his own life. He was only 59.

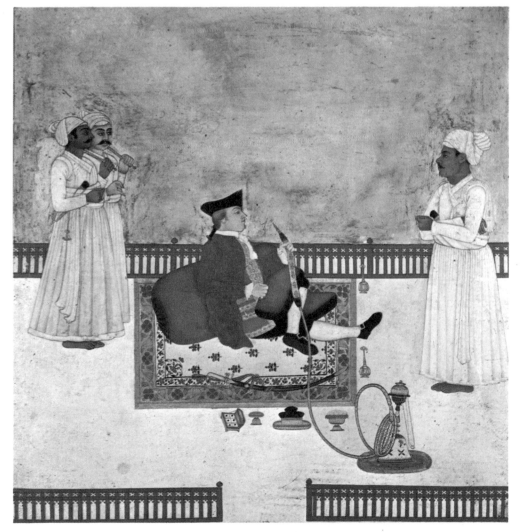

A British official, attended by servants, takes a smoke in Eastern style. Calcutta, Madras and Bombay, with their subordinate factories, were the main centres for the merchants officials, clerks and military personnel employed by the East India Company. They tended to live in style on the proceeds of private trading and use their position to extract gifts; increasingly, because of their military and financial success they came to look on themselves as a superior race. When these rich "nabobs" came home and put on similar airs, they became highly unpopular.

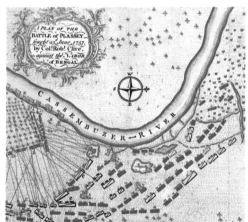

Plan of the Battle of Plassey: Clive's tiny force is on the left by the walled garden; a vast army forms up against him.

Muhammad Shah, a weakling, one of the last Mogul emperors.

Army and Navy

During this period, Britain was involved in four major wars. Her soldiers landed on fever-infested islands and did garrison duty on remote stations; her sailors engaged the enemy all over the world and blockaded his ports.

But, although they won more battles than they lost, the country treated its armed forces with shocking indifference. Between wars, regiments were disbanded, ships laid up and the men sometimes waited years for their back pay. In wartime, the Press Gang and the "Crimp" roamed the streets to seize anyone to serve His Majesty; the victims were mostly loafers, merchant seamen and drunken riff-raff who, once taken, were forced to serve to the end of the war.

Ill-fed and clothed, miserably paid and subject to most brutal discipline, their lives were often thrown away by incompetent officers. Medical care, pensions and family allowances were practically unknown and the marvellous thing is that ruffians treated with such callous inhumanity should have fought so valiantly in a hundred battles. One can only assume that they possessed enormous toughness and courage.

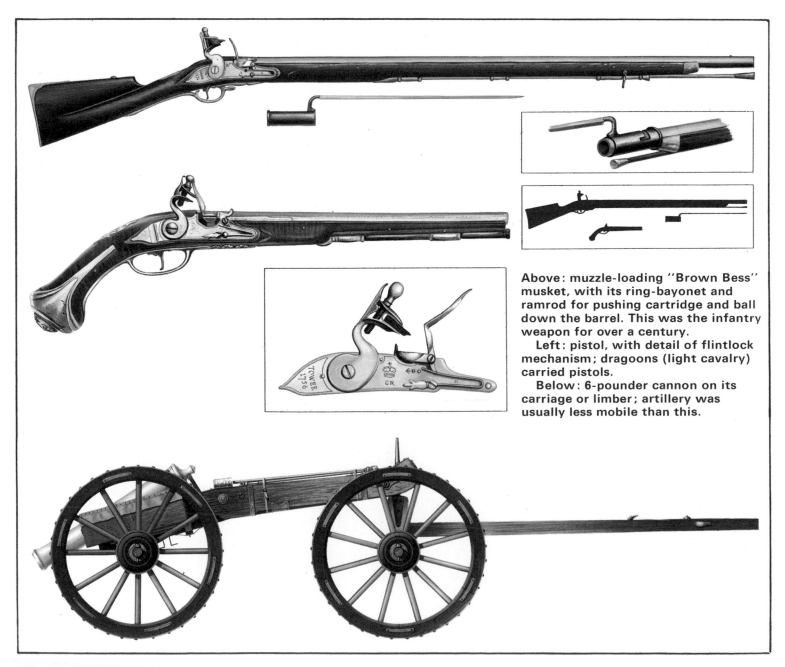

Above: muzzle-loading "Brown Bess" musket, with its ring-bayonet and ramrod for pushing cartridge and ball down the barrel. This was the infantry weapon for over a century.

Left: pistol, with detail of flintlock mechanism; dragoons (light cavalry) carried pistols.

Below: 6-pounder cannon on its carriage or limber; artillery was usually less mobile than this.

The recruiting sergeant is persuading yokels to join up, while accepting a ten-guinea bribe to discharge a soldier.

Sailors

"Our fleets are defrauded by injustice, manned by violence and maintained by cruelty," declared Admiral Vernon. Conditions of service were so bad that the ships could only be manned by means of the Press Gang, which snatched men in sea-faring towns and even boarded merchant-ships. Apart from arrears of pay, the sailors' biggest griev-

The Navy in action: Admiral Vernon's ships of the line put troops ashore to capture Portobello, Panama, 1739. Notice the open gun-ports.

ance was lack of shore leave, but captains knew they would desert. Nevertheless the Navy was proud of its professional skill; officers were trained to make a career at sea and the seamen all believed that they could beat an enemy anywhere in the world.

Soldiers

A man had to be desperate to join the Army. Only crime, drink, bribery or force would induce him to do so. His pay was 8d (just over 3p) a day, out of which he had to pay for food supplied by rascally contractors, and he relied for clothing, quarters and training on his colonel who had bought his promotion and often looked on his regiment as a source of profit.

Regiments consisted of cavalry and foot, for the artillery was a separate service and transport was left to civilians. Marlborough, Amherst and Cumberland introduced better drill and conditions, but discipline still rested on the lash. Those who survived such treatment became the world's finest infantry, renowned for their deadly volleys and steadiness under fire.

Who Governed the Country?

King, Lords and Commons together ruled the country. The King chose his ministers, as a rule, from the House of Lords and the ministers formed the Cabinet to govern Britain. The House of Commons' power lay in its right to vote the taxes and put forward new laws. Moreover, it could claim to speak for the country, even though it was elected by a small number of property-owners. If it chose, it could get rid of an unpopular minister by refusing to grant taxes or by impeachment. Hence, the King and his ministers needed supporters in the Commons.

Walpole, one of the few ministers in the Commons, based his power on support in the House. When he lost it, he resigned and, eventually, this became the recognised conduct, though we later find instances of a minister relying solely on the King's favour.

In theory, the colonies were governed by Britain and subject to the same laws. The King usually appointed a Governor but, in practice, the elected Assemblies had considerable power and they were soon to refuse to obey Westminster.

The corrupt politicians

Land was the key to power, because landowners dominated Parliament. Men entitled to vote in the counties had to hold land worth at least 40 shillings (£2) a year and, in towns, the franchise (vote) went virtually only to property owners. The vast majority of the population had no vote and could only air their views by pamphlets, cartoons and riots.

A lord who owned a borough would hand out jobs, guineas and drink to make sure the electors returned the candidate he wanted. The Duke of Newcastle could put 100 Members into the Commons. A "rotten borough" with very few electors (Old Sarum had seven!) could easily be controlled but, elsewhere, candidates would spend large sums bribing electors and hiring ruffians to intimidate the other side.

Bribes and patronage

Once in Parliament, a Member looked for rewards from his patron —Walpole was expert at providing pensions, jobs in customs, contracts for supplying the Army and grants from the "secret service" fund. "Placemen" could be relied on to vote for the government, for these were the "King's friends", and were rewarded with positions at Court and in the services.

Gillray's cartoon of an election, with a candidate haranguing the crowd, most of whom are there only for the excitement and free drink. Note the woman pouring out gin. Voting lasted several days; there was no secret ballot and electors would openly declare how they would vote. Obviously, a man would not vote against his landlord or employer.

Opposite: the House of Commons in session, in, as you can see by the suits and wigs, the early part of the 18th century. Fortunately, out of 558 Members, about one fifth were dogged independent "country Members" who constantly protested against corruption. Their votes could be decisive and they sometimes removed a minister— even Walpole—from office.

Law and Order

Life in 18th century England, for all its wealth and elegance, was hardly civilised. Crime was rife in the cities, where footpads lurked in the alleys, pickpockets plied their trade and citizens were likely to be robbed and assaulted in broad daylight. Absence of law and order was partly due to the poverty and misery in which a great part of the population lived, but a greater cause was simply the lack of efficient police force and honest magistrates.

Parish constables and a few decrepit watchmen could not cope with determined criminals; unpaid magistrates made a living from taking bribes, and the prisons were few in number, grossly overcrowded and brutally run. In any case, prisons existed for debtors and for those awaiting trial or execution but not, as a rule, to punish or reform offenders.

The authorities' answer to the problem was to make hanging the penalty for most crimes—from murder to poaching. Public hangings were common, but many convicts had their sentences reduced to transportation—to the American colonies for a time and, from 1788, to the new continent of Australia.

A lawyer, with a grinning devil by his side: 18th century lawyers were notorious for their greed and dishonesty.

Daniel Defoe, author of *Robinson Crusoe*, in the pillory in 1702, for writing a religious pamphlet that upset the High Church party and caused him to be sentenced. Crowds usually pelted a prisoner with stones and filth, so he could be badly injured, but Defoe was popular, and the crowd cheered him and brought along flowers and wine.

The Law

There was no Public Prosecutor and a criminal could only be prosecuted if his victim brought the charge. The expense was so great that he often refused to do so.

An accused person came before the Justice of the Peace who, in the country, was probably the Squire but, in cities (especially London), the work of an unpaid magistrate was so dangerous that it was only taken on by scoundrels interested in making money from bribes.

Their offices became known as "Justice Shops", where these "trading Justices" openly sold justice. Constables likewise took bribes from criminals, so it was no wonder that Horace Walpole declared "the greatest criminals in this town are the officers of justice".

Public executions

By 1760, there were over 150 offences for which a person could be hanged. Magistrates often refused to convict for petty offences, but over 100 hangings took place every year in London alone. Vast crowds would collect in a holiday mood to see the victims "turned off" at Tyburn, and rich persons would hire seats in windows overlooking the gallows.

Prisons

Conditions in London's prisons, such as the Marshalsea, the Fleet (for debtors), the King's Bench, Newgate and Bridewell, were horrifying. Prisoners of all types, young and old, were herded together in stinking, insanitary rooms and courtyards, without fresh air, clean water or heating.

Half-naked men and women fought for scraps of food which might be thrown them, for only those with money could obtain meals, ample drink and bedding. Brutal wardens, who bought their positions, demanded fees from prisoners, and those who could not pay suffered appalling treatment and starvation.

A line of chained convicts, including two boys, embarking for the old ships known as the "hulks", which were moored in the Thames at Woolwich. They served as prisons until a fleet assembled to transport the convicts to penal colonies.

The men's sick ward at Marshalsea Prison. Jail fever was rife in all prisons and in one year alone, 3,000 died in the Marshalsea.

A "Charley", one of the watchmen who were supposed to keep law and order by patrolling the streets at night, equipped with stick, rattle and lantern.

The Police

Each year, Justices of the Peace chose a reliable man to act as High Constable for the parish, and he would appoint constables who, whether they liked it or not, had to serve for one year. They were assisted by the Watch, popularly known as "Charlies", mostly poor old men who were fit for little more than calling out the time during the hours of darkness.

Constables, serving unwillingly and for so short a time, received awards for making arrests—£40 for a highwayman, £1 for an army deserter and so on —and they were helped by professional "thief-takers" who acted as informers.

The first real improvement in law and order in London came when Henry Fielding was appointed magistrate at the Bow Street office. Unlike most Justices, Fielding was honest; he asked the public to help him with information and he trained a small band of constables and kept them on when their year was ended. These were the Bow Street Runners. Henry was succeeded by his brother, John, who founded the Bow Street Horse Patrol to deal with highwaymen, and he issued a circular of wanted criminals for magistrates all over the country.

By the end of the century, London had seven magistrates' offices with a few paid Justices and paid constables. Yet, there still existed much opposition to the idea of a regular police force.

The Church

Religion in the 18th century was not the burning force it had been in the previous century. Men and women no longer fought and died for their beliefs, nor were they made to suffer savage penalties for religion's sake.

A Protestant monarchy had been settled by Parliament and, while there still existed laws aimed against Dissenters, Catholics and Jews, these were seldom enforced to the full. By the Test Act, Dissenters were not supposed to hold public positions but almost every year an act was passed to override this ban. The truth was that people had grown tired of religious strife; "enthusiasm", as it was called, was out of date, and the Church of England settled down into a comfortable sort of slumber.

It held its services, went through the forms of religion, but carried out no missionary work among the poor and the ignorant masses. In mid-century, this genteel indolence was disturbed by John Wesley and his followers who went into the open air to preach the Gospel and to bring hope and faith to thousands whom the Church had ignored.

The Mytre in one hand and league in t'other, Shew that the Tubster is a fickle Brother.

Religion in politics: a playing-card of Anne's reign, deriding Dr Sacheverell, a High Church clergyman, who preached against the Whigs.

The Church of England served the Establishment, that is, the ruling class and the well-to-do, and showed little concern for less fortunate folk. Its income was large and hundreds of clergymen enjoyed comfortable livings without needing to show a trace of religious zeal. While the parson hunted, dined or studied his books, parish work was neglected, and in the industrial towns it scarcely existed.

An 18th century cartoon which implies that greedy fat-bellied parsons were riding the Church to its death.

John Wesley preaches from the porch of Trewint Cottage in Cornwall. Cornish folk, especially the tin-miners, took enthusiastically to Methodism.

Foundation of a Methodist chapel: Wesley himself never left the Church of England and did not want Methodism to be another nonconformist sect.

The Methodist revival

John Wesley was born in 1703, the son of an Anglican parson, and he went to Oxford University where he, too, was ordained into the Church. A lively personality, John enjoyed himself at dances, at the theatre and with the ladies, but he also studied hard and came to feel that the Church was failing in its duty towards the poor and had lost its power to inspire men's minds.

"The Bible Moths"

At Oxford, Wesley and his brother, Charles, founded a society for prayer and good works which the undergraduates scoffingly nicknamed "the Bible Moths" or "the Methodists", and the name stuck. Still uncertain of his role in life, John sailed to America to serve as a missionary in the newly-formed state of Georgia, where he had little success with the hard-bitten colonists and the Indians. However, he met some Moravians, members of a German sect, and was deeply impressed by their faith in Christ's power to redeem sin.

Wesley's mission

Back in London Wesley was attending a religious meeting when he suddenly felt he trusted in Christ alone to take away his sins and to bring him salvation. He now had a mission in life and a faith that was to inspire him through every difficulty and hardship. He knew that he must carry the teachings of Christ into the lives of his fellow men.

The great campaign

With his brother Charles and a clergyman named George Whitefield, Wesley began to preach the message of salvation. At first, they preached in churches, but parsons became unwilling to lend their pulpits to men who spoke with such fiery zeal.

So they took to the open air, holding meetings in fields and on village greens but mostly in the towns where many of the poor had never heard of Christ. Small groups of listeners grew into vast crowds and so moving were the hymns that Charles Wesley wrote and so thrilling was the preaching of Whitefield, that rough men would sob aloud and even fall to the ground in agonies of fear and repentance.

In the early days, Wesley's condemnation of worldly pleasures aroused anger, and mobs were stirred up to attack him and his followers. But he would face them fearlessly and walk into their midst to quieten their jeers by his own calm certainty of his power to win them over.

250,000 miles

For over 50 years, until his death in 1791, Wesley travelled 5,000 miles a year, on foot and on horseback. He faced angry mobs and indignant magistrates, he endured hunger and discomfort, storms, floods and riots, in order to preach. As he rode, he read in the saddle, wrote books and letters to encourage his friends and train preachers to carry on his work. Nothing, except death, could stop him.

Methodism

The effects of this tremendous campaign were to bring hope, comfort and self-respect to tens of thousands of people, especially the poor and the

Wesley in the midst of a riot. He once described how he felt when in danger: "my heart was filled with love, my mouth with arguments. They were ashamed, they were melted down."

ignorant. As Wesley hoped, it also awoke the Church of England to its duty and it founded, to Wesley's regret, a new Church.

Methodism spread widely in the United States where its clear message made a ready appeal to people, many of whose ancestors had emigrated for religion's sake.

The Good Household

Britain's population was still remarkably small. In 1700, England was reckoned to have 5½ million inhabitants, a third of the number in France. Yet this small nation played a leading role in the world, partly because its people were lively and pugnacious and also because of its social make-up.

It was a much freer society than in most Continental countries, and its upper ranks were never closed to those who had the luck or ability to climb. A man might build up a small business, so that his son could add to it and prosper, buy an estate, educate his sons like gentlemen and see his well-dowered daughters marry into the county families. Younger sons of the nobility often took up careers in business; this was necessary because the eldest son inherited the whole estate, apart from "portions" (lump sums) to his brothers and dowries to his sisters.

It was an easy-going society, with a great deal more freedom for women than they were to know in the following century: "they do whatsoever they please", remarked a foreigner, "and do generally wear the breeches".

The Georgian household

The home of a prosperous shop-keeper or lawyer stood solid and dignified in red brick or white stucco. It contained dining-parlour, drawing-room and perhaps a study for the master; beyond and at the back, were the "offices"—kitchen, pantries, china-closet, wash-house and sometimes a brewery.

Upstairs consisted of four or five bedrooms and the garrets or attics where the servants slept. There was no bathroom nor, as a rule, any water-closet, only a privy in the garden or some dark corner.

Servants

Even a modest household included three or four servants who lived in—a personal man, a housemaid and scullery-maid. Often, there was a house-boy and a gardener as well. Capable housewives, with help from the servants, saw to their own baking, brewing, preserving and butter-making; they made feather-beds, pillows, candles, ink and soap at home.

Servants' wages were rising, so a housemaid would earn £4 or £5 a year and her keep, a man would receive £6 to £10 and a suit. Parson Woodforde in 1783 paid out £22 10s 6d (£22.52½) in wages to his five servants, though the boy had only 10s 6d (52½p). Though there was a good deal of grumbling about laziness and insolence, servants were regarded as part of the family; often, they stayed on for years, were rewarded with gifts and beaten when they misbehaved.

Meals

Meals began with breakfast, taken at perhaps ten o'clock, usually no more than bread and butter and tea. Dinner time had moved forward to two or three in the afternoon and even to five. Supper, consisting of the cold meats, was eaten at ten at night and, with dinner, was the only other considerable meal. Since they consumed so many meats, puddings, tarts, wines and other drinks, it is not surprising that people ate only once or twice a day.

A Georgian kitchen scene (above), with a large joint being basted by the cook as he turns the spit. Water had to be fetched from the well and wood chopped to keep the fire going. Most kitchens still had an open fireplace, with the fire on the hearth and a brick oven at the side.

A country family sits down to a plain dinner in the kitchen (opposite), with none of the plenty of middle-class households; these belong to the pious, hard-working class of small farmers of whom a traveller wrote, "They fare extremely hard . . . and practise every lesson of diligence and frugality."

The Rich

The Age of Elegance was also the Age of Privilege. The greater part of the country's wealth was in the hands of a comparatively small number of landowners and merchants. While magnates like the Newcastles, the Bedfords, Rockinghams and Devonshires lived like kings and were literally as rich as some continental monarchs, the bulk of the population was desperately poor. A successful merchant might make £20,000 a year, when a workman would be lucky to earn £20. What was the effect of this top-heavy distribution of wealth?

Some of those who possessed colossal incomes spent their money on reckless extravagance and gambling; some invested it in order to produce still greater wealth. They sunk mines, built ironworks, factories, canals and bridges, drained marshes and improved the farming land.

Many of the wealthy devoted their riches to elegance and beauty. They built magnificent houses and filled them with exquisite furnishings, paintings, and artistic treasures, but it was only the unequal sharing of wealth that brought these splendours into existence.

The shepherdess, an exquisite porcelain statuette, made in the Chelsea factory in 1769. The art of making figures in porcelain (translucent pottery) came originally from China and, by the 18th century, was carried out in Germany (e.g. Meissen), France (Sèvres), Italy and England, where the Chelsea, Bow, Derby, Worcester and Rockingham factories produced some beautiful objects.

A bed designed by Thomas Chippendale in the Chinese style which, for a time from about 1760, became all the rage. Chairs, staircases, wallpapers and summer-houses were specially made to meet this strange fashion.

A magnificent panel doorway in Northumberland House, designed by Robert Adam, the leading architect of his day. He drew his ideas from Roman art and used classical decoration and delicate colours.

Artistic taste

The rich went to enormous pains to fill their houses with beautiful things. Noblemen would import porcelain and wallpaper from China, would pick up art treasures all over Europe, or spend a small fortune buying Renaissance Old Masters.

The finest craftsmen in the country, working under some acknowledged master like Chippendale, were employed to make superb furniture; fireplaces and doorways were designed like works of art and Italian experts were brought over to decorate ceilings.

Good taste and elegance became hallmarks of the period, which is surprising in view of the gentry's limited education in school. However, most young men of quality made the Grand Tour, travelling for a year or two through France into Italy, with visits perhaps to Germany, and farther afield. Not only did they see great art collections, but they polished their manners and broadened their ideas through mixing with the highest society in Europe.

Above: the country gentleman and his lady: a portrait of Mr and Mrs Andrews, painted by Thomas Gainsborough, who catches to perfection the arrogant self-assurance of this elegant couple, who, with their estate stretching into the distance, know their position in society.

Below: a more critical view of the upper class by William Hogarth who shows them, in the midst of luxurious surroundings, to be indolent, bored and vulgar. Notice the hairdresser; also the negro servant and boy, fashionable additions to a wealthy household.

The Poor

In terms of housing, clothes and food, the entire working-class was poor, but there were degrees of poverty. Craftsmen like silversmiths and tailors, along with superior servants, were better off than most wage-earners, like miners, shipwrights and foundrymen.

Cottage weavers, stocking-knitters and nail-makers lived at the mercy of the merchants who supplied raw materials and, in the country, where enclosures had taken a man's bit of land and grazing rights, farmworkers existed on starvation wages eked out by earnings of wives and children. Town labourers, porters, hawkers, scullery-maids and rag-pickers earned what little they could and, at the bottom of society, a mass of destitute wretches lived out their short lives in misery.

The Elizabethan Poor Law system, designed to cope with a smaller, more settled population, no longer worked. The problem was too big for parish authorities with only small sums to spend on poor relief, and, in any case, poverty was considered a natural state of life. Low wages and dear food were thought necessary to make the lower classes work hard.

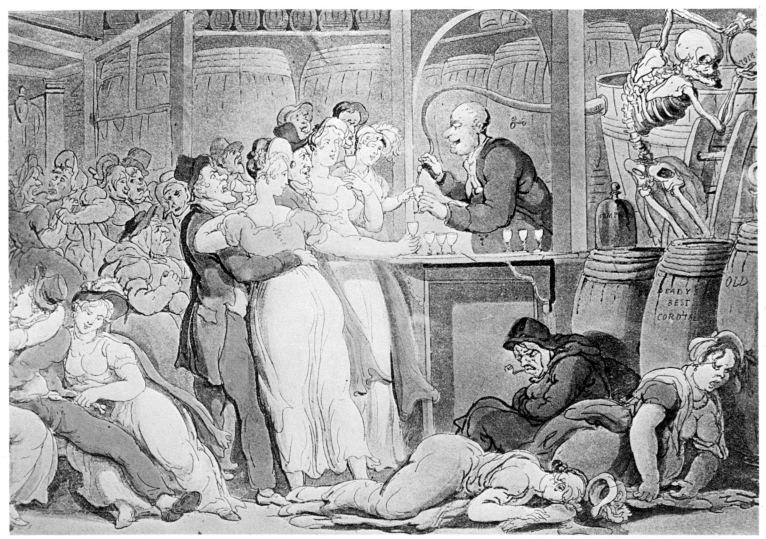

Gin-drinking

From about 1700, the technique of distilling gin from grain became well-known and production of spirits rose steeply. Thousands of "dram shops" did roaring business, for gin was very cheap and, perhaps to forget their misery, the poor took to gin-drinking with a kind of mania.

The increase in violence, crime, degradation and death shocked people even in this hard-drinking age. In 1751,

The Dram Shop by Rowlandson: on "demon gin", a man could get drunk for a penny, dead-drunk for twopence.

an Act was passed to tax spirits and, from then on, drunkenness slowly declined.

The Foundling Hospital (above), opened in Hatton Garden in 1740, by Thomas Coram, who was shocked by the numbers of destitute children in London. Parishes put abandoned babies in workhouses or farmed them out to so-called "nurses".

Charterhouse (left), another London institution for the poor. Originally a monastery, it came into the hands of Thomas Sutton who left money to maintain a school and an almshouse for 80 poor old men.

A chimney-sweep with his "climbing boy". Babies who survived the workhouse were apprenticed at the age of seven, the parish paying about £5 per boy to a master who was supposed to teach him a trade. Chimney-sweeps merely wanted a supply of little slaves; fees were low and masters would take on 20 boys, send them out to beg in summer and hire them out for 6d (2½p) a day in winter.

A beggar family: illness, unemployment, death of the breadwinner could reduce a family to destitution; in theory, the parish should help but many persons had moved far from their native parish. Hordes of professional beggars, cripples, blind, wounded soldiers and women with barefoot children (hired for the day), came on to the streets each morning from the alleys of Seven Dials and St Giles in London.

Progress in the Towns

The movement of the people from the country to the towns went on steadily, though it was not yet a headlong scramble. London, it is true, was always growing and, with over half a million inhabitants, was 20 times the size of the next cities in the kingdom, Bristol and Norwich. Thanks to the American trade, Liverpool and Plymouth were thriving; Birmingham was becoming a conglomeration of small industries; Newcastle and Hull prospered on the coal-trade and fish, but many of the smaller towns and ports were static or actually declining in size and importance.

However, dotted about the Midlands and the North were towns humming with new developments; machinery was speeding up cloth-manufacture; iron and coal production was rising and steam-engines were already pumping water from mines. Communications improved, as roads became smoother and new bridges and canals were constructed.

Life in the towns began to be cleaner; the plague no longer came each summer, streets were paved and lit, but the purity of water and safe sewage disposal were yet to be considered.

London in the 18th century: a view of the Stocks Market, with a statue of Charles II in the centre, on the site of the Mansion House. Notice the Wren church, the handsome brick and stucco house: foreigners were astonished by London's splendid buildings and shops. The slums were worse than ever, but, to the west, fine squares, streets and crescents were built and two new bridges crossed the Thames at Blackfriars and Westminster.

Improvements in town

In the better parts of town and city, paving-stones replaced the old cobbles, open gutters down the middle disappeared, garbage was regularly cleared away, houses began to be numbered and the new oil street lamps shone bravely from dusk until midnight.

Water from Hertfordshire was brought 20 miles into London in pipes made from elm-trunks; a reservoir was built at Islington and many houses now had cisterns and lead piping.

The rich installed water-closets in their homes, but, since sewage seeped into wells or was emptied into the Thames and this was still a main source of household water, outbreaks of typhoid were regular occurrences.

Below: A high-wire artist performs in Islington Gardens, while fireworks light the sky and an orchestra plays in the pavilion or Rotunda, for the entertainment of lords, ladies, shopkeepers, clerks and milliners. London had a number of these gardens—Vauxhall and Ranelagh were the most fashionable but there were many others where, for an entrance-fee, people of all classes could enjoy an evening out, strolling along the covered walks, eating and drinking in arbours and pavilions, while watching the performers and listening to music.

People at Work

Throughout all the upheavals that had taken place since 1603, men had steadily gone on finding better ways to produce coal, iron and manufactured goods of every kind. By the start of the 18th century, Britain was already one of the most industrialised countries in Europe and it soon began to forge ahead of its rivals. There were several reasons for this.

In overtaking the Dutch, Englishmen learned much about finance and the building of canals, ships and dockyards. The Navigation Laws (by which goods had mostly to be carried in English ships) fostered ship-building; wars encouraged higher production of metals, leather goods and cloth. Higher customs duty on imported goods caused the English to produce their own silk, sail-cloth, linen and paper.

The first Lancashire blast-furnaces were built because foreign iron was too dear, and tinplate was produced in Wales to replace German imports. The Royal Society's reports to encourage better machines helped mechanical engineering to develop and a spate of inventions came into use. By mid-century, the Industrial Revolution had already dawned.

Providing for and employing all the Poor in Gr. Britain.

The Poor when manag'd, and employ'd in Trade,
Are to the publick Welfare, usefull made;
But if kept Idle from their Vices spring
Whores for the Stews, and Soldiers for the King.

A playing-card showing the so-called "vices" of the unemployed—playing games, quarrelling, drinking and chatting.

Poverty

Unemployment and poverty were widespread (hence the huge servant class) but, though wealth was shared unequally, not much could be done about it. The country simply did not yet produce enough jobs or wealth for everyone. But, by this time, famines were unknown and the Poor Law gave better help than in most countries.

A pit-head in England at the end of the century: notice the use of horses and mules for transport, the winding-gear on the right and pumping-machine in the centre. In about 1700, Britain's coal-industry, producing 2½ million tons a year, was the biggest in the world but, as pits went deeper, water was a problem. By 1712, Newcomen had perfected a steam-pumping-engine to drain mines; it used enormous amounts of fuel but this was no problem at pit-heads. James Watt's steam-engine, perfected in 1769, was much more efficient.

The metal industries

A major breakthrough occurred around 1700 when a method was discovered of using coke instead of charcoal to smelt lead and copper ore. Lead-smelting developed in Wales and the Pennines, with a copper-smelting industry around Bristol, using ore from Cornwall and coal from Shropshire. The brass industries of Birmingham benefitted from this new activity.

In 1709, Abraham Darby succeeded in producing coke-smelted iron at a furnace in Coalbrookdale, Shropshire, and the new process spread to Wales and the Black Country.

A French observer thought that Britain's naval victories were due to her cannon, made from coke-smelted iron, being superior to the French guns.

Machines for the cotton industry

A ban on the import of Indian calicoes helped cotton manufacture to get going in Lancashire. Demand for cotton goods was so great that faster production was needed and John Kay's Flying Shuttle (1733) enabled one weaver to do the work of two.

This called for swifter spinning, and Hargreaves' Spinning Jenny (1760) began with eight spindles instead of one, and later used 120 spindles, though it was a hand-worked machine which could be installed in cottages. Later developments meant that it was only a matter of time before textiles were produced in factories, instead of in people's homes.

Before the Industrial Revolution: Wensleydale knitters at work outside their houses. For centuries, cloth production depended upon spinners and weavers working in their cottages. It was the invention of machines needing non-human power that led to the factory system.

Children at work in a rope-factory. At this time, people did not look on child-labour as a shocking hardship, but as a welcome chance for the poor to earn money to feed themselves.

Nant-y-Glo Ironworks in Wales, an early example of ugly squalor, yet the new industries brought work to some of the poorest farming areas.

Workshop into factory

At the beginning of this era, the normal type of manufacturing business was a small workshop where a master-craftsman employed a few workers and apprentices to turn raw materials into locks, tools, fire-grates and so on. Middlemen supplied the materials and took back the finished articles at agreed rates.

Matthew Boulton (1728–1809), a hardware manufacturer, decided to launch out on a bigger scale and, in 1762, he opened a factory, the Soho Works, Birmingham, where 600 to 800 workers were employed making various articles of metal and glass with the aid of water-driven machinery.

People at Play

The 18th century saw the beginnings of organised sport. A wealthy class needed to occupy its leisure, particularly in the country, and sports like horse-racing, cricket and boxing now began to have sets of rules. This was chiefly due to the heavy gambling that went on. When a man bet £100 on the result of a prize fight or a cricket match, he wanted to know the rules of the contest.

The gentry became patrons of sport, putting up the prizes, owning the horses and employing jockeys, athletes and prize-fighters; some of them also boxed and rode with the paid "professional" sportsmen. This was particularly true of cricket, in which a team might include lord, squire, parson, farm labourers and, as captain, his lordship's gardener.

A more civilised attitude to animals caused bull and bear-baiting to die out. Those with less energetic tastes attended the pleasure-gardens, masked balls, fireworks displays and fairs, where fashionable society rubbed shoulders with ordinary citizens, but in general it was only the well-to-do classes who could afford these sports and amusements.

The Rotunda, House and Gardens at Ranelagh in May 1759, during a fashionable Ball. Many of the guests are in fancy dress, some dancing round a maypole.

An eye-witness account

Ranelagh lay on the opposite side of the river to its rival, Vauxhall. In 1742, Horace Walpole wrote, "Two nights ago, the gardens opened at Chelsea; the Prince, Princess, the Duke of Cumberland, much nobility and much mob were there. There is a vast amphitheatre, finely gilt, painted and illuminated into which everybody that loves eating, drinking, staring or crowding is admitted for twelve pence." A masquerade was "the prettiest spectacle that ever I saw . . . when you entered you found the whole garden spread with tents . . . a maypole dressed with garlands and people dancing around it . . . all masked, as were the various bands of music."

A game of quoits (left), with a bowling green in the background. In quoits, players threw heavy iron rings at a peg or "hob".

A lady cricketer of 1779 (below)—a skit on women's invasion of sport. Cricket's rules were first drafted in 1744, when bowling was underarm, and the wicket had only two stumps.

Prize-fighting with bare fists. The contestants fought for a "purse", put up by some nobleman, and fights lasted 60, 100 or more rounds, a round ending only with a knock-down; the fight ended when one man could no longer rise. Until 1743, when Jack Broughton introduced rules of boxing, a man could hit his opponent where and how he pleased and could seize him round the waist and throw him down.

Houses (1)

The 18th century was a golden age of architecture. It began with the gracious homely style of Queen Anne, when rectangular houses of brick were built with sloping roofs, sturdy chimneys and large regularly-spaced windows.

Then, from about 1715, came the Palladian style, based on the buildings of classical Rome; architects like Lord Burlington, Colen Campbell and William Kent designed houses according to strict rules, and a Palladian mansion such as Holkham Hall had a grand central block, an impressive portico and supporting wings containing stables and kitchens.

Robert Adam introduced delicate, more elegant touches to relieve the coldness of the classical style and much attention was paid to "landscaping", so the house stood in a "natural" setting of trees and lakes.

The smaller, Georgian house was plain to look at, with little ornament, other than a fine doorway which often had a pillared porch; windows and chimneys were carefully spaced to give a feeling of balance. Public buildings and churches also expressed the people's liking for buildings with a solid, prosperous air.

Low Middleton Hall, County Durham (above), a fine Queen Anne house in pink brick with large symmetrically-placed windows.

The beautifully proportioned Palladian Bridge (left) in the grounds of Wilton House, Wiltshire.

Holkham Hall, Norfolk, a Palladian mansion, built for Thomas Coke, a wealthy young man who spent ten years on the Grand Tour. Lord Burlington and his "school" worked out the design and William Kent was architect-in-chief. The dun brick exterior is grand rather than attractive but the interior of the house is magnificent.

Cound Hall, Shropshire (above), built early in Queen Anne's reign: a tall solid house, rather severe in style.

Pallant House, Chichester (left), a Georgian town house with a fine doorway.

Town architecture

A feature of Georgian town architecture was the beginning of what we now call town-planning. In the growing towns and the new suburbs of London, land-owners would put up whole streets, squares and crescents as part of an architectural design, instead of as separate buildings. A terrace, built in the Georgian style, might contain 12 or 20 dwellings, all with identical doors and windows, so that the whole row was impressive and pleasing in a way that 20 separate houses could never be.

Crescents and town squares were often given ornamental iron balconies and handsome iron railings; sometimes the ends and centre of a terrace had pillars and pediments, and classical urns might be placed along the parapet, all to emphasise that this was a single unit of architecture.

Each house in the terrace was tall and narrow, usually the width of a single room. The front door opened into a hall with the stairs leading upwards in a series of dog-leg turns or sometimes in a fine curved sweep; the dining-room, large, lofty and well-lit by its high windows, was on the ground-floor above the basement kitchen, while the drawing-room was on the first-floor. Bedrooms came higher still, with the servants' attics at the very top.

The Circus, Bath (above), by John Wood the Elder (1754), a superb example of houses designed as a unit.

Hanover Square, London (below), with Georgian town-houses built in the formal, dignified style.

Houses (2)

Great care was taken to make the inside of a house as impressive as its exterior. Architects designed interiors down to the last detail and engaged craftsmen to carry out their ideas.

Doors, fireplaces and ceilings were designed in the supposed style of ancient Rome. Walls were hung with Italian velvets and silks or painted in delicate colours with ornamental mouldings that echoed the ceiling's design. Columns, slender pillars and curved niches would give the salon or library the appearance of a classical temple.

Furniture was arranged against the walls to leave the middle of the room clear for people to admire the pictures, to converse and display their fine clothes. Each chair, sofa and side-table had its appointed place; a row of chairs might make a band of colour or a writing desk would exactly fit its own alcove. In dining-rooms, it was not usual for a table to occupy the centre; servants would bring in a gate-leg table or several tripod tables and serve food from marble-topped side-tables with handsome mirrors above.

A grandfather clock (left), whose magnificent case was designed in the classical style.

Chippendale doll's house (above); a miniature Georgian town-house with entrance hall, kitchen, parlours, etc.

Furniture-makers

The most famous names in furniture making are Chippendale, Hepplewhite and Sheraton, a trio of Englishmen who, in the latter part of the 18th century, produced a great variety of chairs, settees, writing-desks and tables. Chippendale, a businessman with a keen eye for changing fashions, influenced Hepplewhite whose work was noted for its graceful curves.

Sheraton returned to straight lines

The Breakfast Room by Hogarth (opposite), in the Palladian style of William Kent, but the furniture is Queen Anne period, solid and less elegant than that of the second half of the century.

and made much use of decoration, carving, brass handles and inlays. All three wrote books and so, with *The Cabinet Maker's and Upholsterer's Guide* in front of him, a humble market-town joiner could make a set of Hepplewhite chairs in the gracious style of the master.

Queen Anne wing chair (above) with embroidered wool upholstery.

Robert Adam room at Osterley Park, Middlesex (left). Notice the matching patterns on walls and ceiling, the classical urns, statues, doorway and flat columns.

The World of Fashion

The wealth of the English upper classes created new standards of elegance and sophistication in the country. The young men who made the Grand Tour brought back the refined tastes of continental high society and the fashions of France. Money was made to be spent and the wealthy lavished it upon every whim and luxury, from gilt chandeliers and Sèvres porcelain to Negro servants and extravagant finery in dress. Nothing in the way of embroidery, lace, silver-gilt or fantastic hair-styles was too expensive; no craftsman, whether he was a woodcarver of genius, like Grinling Gibbons or an artist like Reynolds, was too costly to hire.

Yet, this new-found elegance was in some ways artificial. It went hand-in-hand with a coarseness and vulgarity which could be seen all too easily in table-manners and gluttony, in the outspoken language even of Court and drawing-room and in the uncontrollable tempers that led to so many brawls and duels. The English possessed none of the national culture of the French and the Italians who continued to be amazed and amused by the antics of the pugnacious islanders.

Right: a cartoon poking fun at ladies' hairstyles and their absurd gentlemen friend—a fop, known as a "macaroni". Hair was drawn up over a frame stuffed with wool, then greased, powdered and decorated. This style was both unhygenic and uncomfortable.

Below: Hogarth's young man in fashionable London where, among fops, braggarts and worldly old gentlemen, he waits to attend a Court function. Notice the various styles of wigs and coats, the cocked hat on the left, the old man's tricorne and the young man's turban resembling a nightcap. The younger men display fine linen or lace at throat and cuffs, a fashion of which the older men do not approve.

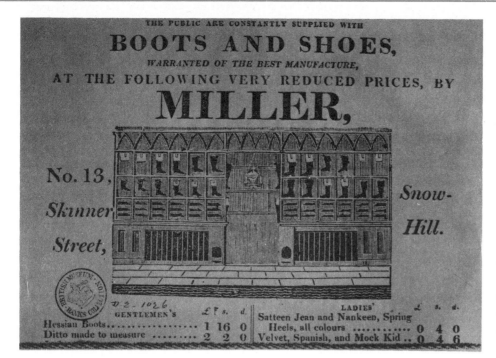

Shops

Shops were much fewer than now and their small bow-fronted windows could not display many goods. Price-tickets were unknown, and customers would strike a bargain with the shopkeeper. His assistants still lived in and worked long hours, for the candle-lit shops stayed open until 10 pm.

Country shops mostly sold locally-made goods and a consignment of, say, drapery from London would cause lively excitement. Ready-made clothes were now coming in and there was a big trade in second-hand clothes passed down to the street dealers.

There was a tax on newspaper advertisements, so shopkeepers issued trade cards like this one.

A brocaded dress (i.e. one with a raised pattern) of 1745–50. Primrose or yellow was a fashionable colour and the decoration takes the form of sprays of leaves and flowers arranged in an artfully casual manner. Silk brocades had earlier been much heavier, but, as skirts became fuller, delicate colours and widely-spaced designs prevented the dress from looking enormous. This one has an elegant simplicity and no detail except the elbow cuffs. High corsets were no longer worn to push up the bust and genteel ladies' figures now looked much flatter.

Changing fashions

In Marlborough's time, men wore a long coat with full skirts over a sleeveless buttoned waistcoat, so long it hid the tight breeches; square-toed shoes were adorned with bows. Every man of quality wore a large wig.

Gradually, the coat became less full and the waistcoat shorter to reveal knee-breeches, with silk stockings below and buckled shoes. Wigs were much smaller, with bunches of curls at the side and a tail at the back, while three-cornered hats were smaller. Later, the brim would be fastened to the crown in two places to make a "cocked hat".

Hooped skirts came back for ladies in about 1720. The skirt, divided in front to show an embroidered underskirt, was stretched over a frame at the sides, and it became so wide that it was impossible for two ladies to pass on pavement or staircase. Then came in a version hinged at the waist, so one side or both could be raised to pass through doorways.

Materials, such as taffetas, damasks and muslins, were much lighter than brocades. Waists were tight and long, with low-cut bodices often laced down the front with ribbons, and half-sleeves revealing lace ruffles.

Neat powdered hairstyles changed in the late '60s to fantastic constructions, crowned with ribbons, flowers and even model ships!

The Agricultural Revolution (1)

At the opening of the century, half the working population was employed on the land and, with blacksmiths, wheelwrights, harness-makers, corn-merchants, butchers, carriers and those like doctors and shopkeepers who served them, some three-quarters of the population earned its living from the land. Why then should there have been an agricultural "revolution"?

The population was increasing and, with developments in commerce and industry, more people were going to live in towns and more food was needed to feed them. Bigger demand meant bigger profits for energetic farmers and so we find improvements in sowing seed and tending crops, in the management or rotation of crops, in manuring and draining, in breeding bigger and healthier animals. But, from the farmers' point of view, the biggest improvement was to do away with the old open-field system and to make separate farms with fields enclosed by hedges and fences. This took time, and the word "revolution" is probably wrong, for it implies violent changes. What happened was agricultural "evolution", a slow steady process of change.

Frontispiece of Blagrave's *Epitome of the Art of Husbandry* (summary of farm management) published in 1669. The pictures illustrate tree-pruning, bird-scaring, harvesting and tulip-growing —there was a mania for these flowers and bulbs. Trapping birds and fish were evidently important activities, too. At this time, farming was making steady progress, especially in corn production and drainage of water-logged land, and the 18th century improvements must be seen as a continuation of earlier methods.

The butcher offers his customers his finest beef, fed on oil-cake, a new kind of cattle-feed. The gentleman would be content with second-best meat, but his wife declares she will have "Sir Loin of Nobility", the very best cut.

Meat

The cartoon above illustrates the abundance of meat in the markets. This came about because sheep and cattle doubled in size during the century and much more winter-killed meat was available.

Breeders like Robert Bakewell pointed to the way in which better animals could be produced by selecting only the healthiest for breeding, and this could not be done until farmers could keep their beasts in enclosed fields instead of having to run them with poor quality animals on the open commons and wastes.

Fodder, such as turnips, swedes, and oil-cake, meant that stock no longer had to be killed off in the autumn, so supplies of fresh meat were available all the year round.

A giant Lincolnshire bull, painted by George Stubbs, the famous painter of horses and cattle, who has exaggerated the bull's size by placing it in the foreground so that the farmer looks like a pygmy.

Cotswold sheep, almost rectangular in shape and, again, exaggerated in size. Sheep now came to be bred chiefly for their wool or for mutton, for it was rarely possible to produce a top-quality dual-purpose animal.

Farming people

People involved in farming belonged to one of three groups. The big land-owners drew their incomes from letting out land to tenants, though they usually kept a home farm to produce food for the great house and also to indulge in the fashionable occupation of experimental farming.

The second group, the farmers, varied greatly in wealth. Some owned their land and lived like the gentry; others struggled along hardly better off than cottagers. Generally speaking, the tenant-farmers did better than small owners who had to pay land-tax and lacked capital for improvements.

The third group, the labourers, were either farm-servants who were hired for the year and lived in at the farm, or were day-labourers, living in a cottage with a garden and the right to graze a cow and keep a few hens on the common. Earning only about 8d to 1s (3p–5p) a day and nothing in wet weather, these labourers could only exist with the help of the small earnings of their wives and children.

Farming improvements

Improvements in farming came when a man no longer farmed a number of scattered strips but had his land in one compact farm. Then he could improve the land by deep ploughing or draining, by manuring or marling (adding clay to light soil); he could fatten his cattle by feeding them in stalls in his new cow-shed and he could grow fodder crops like turnips and clover instead of leaving land to lie fallow.

Fodder provided winter feed and clover actually improved the soil for subsequent grain crops. More fodder meant more beasts, more manure, more fertile land, better crops and better profits to pay for further improvements.

Portrait of Robert Bakewell (1725–95) who farmed at Dishley in Leicestershire. Through studying selective breeding, he originated the Leicester breed of sheep but was less successful with cattle. He made a fortune from hiring out his Leicester rams.

The Agricultural Revolution (2)

The single most important improvement in farming during the 18th century was enclosure. To some extent, this had been going on for many, many years, but now it became a regular policy to change open fields, commons and wastes into compact farms.

A landlord who wished to enclose land held on the old open-field system would propose an Enclosure Bill, with compensation for the villagers who were to lose their land and rights to pasturage and wood-cutting. When this had been agreed (generally to the landlord's advantage), Parliament passed without question an Enclosure Act to make the business legal. Between 1714 and 1720, five Enclosure Acts were passed, but the numbers rose to 204 in 1741–60 and to 1,043 in 1761–80.

In place of the old system of peasants growing food by wasteful methods, the land could now be cultivated in larger units and in more efficient ways. More food would be produced for a growing population but, on the other side of the picture, thousands of country folk lost their holdings and became landless labourers or took themselves off to the towns.

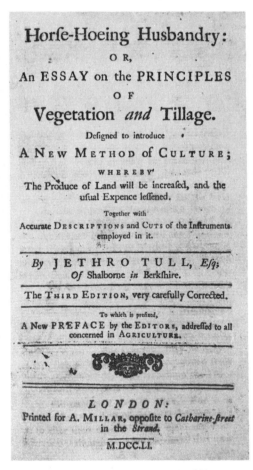

Frontispiece of Jethro Tull's *Horse-hoeing Husbandry,* first published in 1733. Tull, a Berkshire farmer, devised a drill for sowing seeds in rows instead of broadcast. Weeds could then be kept down by hoeing between the rows with a horse-drawn hoe. He wrote his book in answer to attacks on his theories, some of which were quite wrong.

How to make a manure-pit; from a farming book of 1756.

Farmyard manure

Artificial fertilisers were not yet available to farmers and the traditional method of enriching land had been to graze sheep and cattle across the stubble after harvest.

When cattle were stall-fed and numbers of farm horses were kept, manure (dung mixed with bedding-straw) had to be collected and stored, for it was more valuable when rotted down. This was best done in pits, because a heap exposed to rain lost some of its goodness. When ready, the manure was spread on the fields and ploughed in.

This four Wheel Drill Plow, with a Seed and a Manure Hopper, was first Invented in the Year 174. and is now in Use with Wᵐ Ellis at Little Gaddesden near Hempstead in Hertfordshire. where any persᵒ may View the same. It is so light that a Man may Draw it. but Generally drawn by a pony or little Horse

This machine is described in its advertisement as "a four Wheel Drill Plow, with a Seed and Manure Hopper". But it is not a plough in the usual sense of the word, for the tines at the back, when lowered, can do no more than cover over the seeds dropped from the first of the two hoppers.

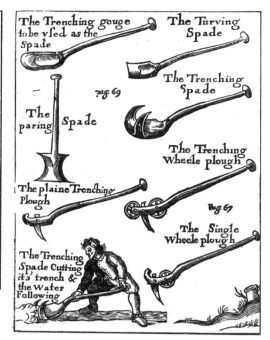

A selection of tools for draining marshy land, from a late 17th century book on agriculture.

Famous farmers

The most celebrated names in the history of farming are Jethro Tull, "Turnip" Townshend, Robert Bakewell and Coke of Holkham, though some modern historians think that they did not deserve their reputations.

However, Tull's drill and horse-hoe brought new machines on the land and made cultivation more efficient, while Lord Townshend (1674–1738), having given up politics after a quarrel with Walpole, took to farming in Norfolk where he may not have introduced turnips, but certainly grew them on a large scale to provide winter feed for cattle. His rotation of wheat, roots, barley and clover abolished the fallow year in the old three-field system.

Bakewell's Leicestershire sheep were bred to produce mutton rather than wool and to do so in two years. Possibly the meat was fat and of low quality, but Bakewell had many imitators and, in his lifetime, Britain's meat supply doubled.

When Coke began farming he said Holkham had "one blade of grass and two rabbits fighting for it". By enriching the soil and building up his flocks, he won such a reputation that crowds came every year to Holkham's sheep-shearing to see his farms.

Thomas Coke (1752–1842) proudly inspects his Southdown sheep at Holkham Hall in Norfolk, the estate which he greatly enriched by scientific farming.

The Writers

Writers in the 18th century generally enjoyed an importance that has seldom been equalled. Whereas, formerly, they had had to rely on some wealthy patron, they now found themselves in favour with governments that needed popular support.

By 1724, there were 16 newspapers in London alone, besides magazines and journals; some authors earned large sums from their writing; Dr Johnson held forth like an emperor to a circle of admirers, and writers like Addison, Steele, Defoe and Swift influenced politics. As "men of letters", they were welcome in polite society and their work and the poems of Dryden and Pope reflect the elegance and heartlessness of that society. Defoe and Swift also used their pens to describe the follies and miseries of the world about them.

As the reading public grew, so there appeared the first great English novels, *Robinson Crusoe* and *Gulliver's Travels*. These were followed by the works of Richardson, Fielding and Smollett, and the novel became by far the most popular form of reading, relying, as it did, upon giving a vivid picture of English life contained in an exciting story.

Gulliver arrives in Lilliput, is captured, transported and put on public show by the little people who, at first, seem attractive, but presently reveal themselves as treacherous and petty-minded.

Satirists

A satire is a piece of verse or prose which aims to improve society by ridiculing its behaviour. The writer usually describes absurd characters behaving in ridiculous ways and he relies on wit and mock seriousness to make the satire bite home.

The 18th century was the great age of English satire, when Pope, Dryden and Johnson wrote in verse. In the *Rape of the Lock*, Pope, writing in witty polished couplets, poked fun at the vanity of fashionable society but, in the *Dunciad*, he was much more venomous in attacking fellow writers.

Jonathan Swift

Swift, disappointed in his hopes of promotion in the Church, and forced to live in Dublin in what he considered to be exile, wrote bitterly about the sufferings of the Irish poor and, in *Gulliver's Travels*, which was never intended as a book for children, he expressed a savage contempt for mankind.

In those weird countries of Lilliput, Brobdingnag and Laputa, Gulliver encounters the greed and cruelty which filled Swift with so much disgust in the real world. The sheer nastiness of human beings depressed him so utterly that towards the end of his life this unhappy genius became insane.

Science-fiction in 1726: on his third voyage, Gulliver reaches Laputa, the flying island which is run by mad scientists who crush all opposition to their rule.

DICTIONARY

OF THE

ENGLISH LANGUAGE:

IN WHICH

The WORDS are deduced from their ORIGINALS,

AND

ILLUSTRATED in their DIFFERENT SIGNIFICATIONS

BY

EXAMPLES from the best WRITERS.

TO WHICH ARE PREFIXED,

A HISTORY of the LANGUAGE,

AND

AN ENGLISH GRAMMAR.

BY SAMUEL JOHNSON, A.M.

IN TWO VOLUMES.

VOL. I.

Title-page of Johnson's Dictionary, published 1755. This great work revealed the author's amazing memory and knowledge, though it lacked understanding of word-origins.

A

Table Alphabeticall, contayning and teaching the true writing and vnderstanding of hard vsuall English words, borrowed from the Hebrew, Greeke, Latine, or French, &c.

With the Interpretation thereof by plaine English words, gathered for the benefit and help of all vnskilfull persons.

Whereby they may the more easily and better vnderstand many hard English words, which they shall heare or read in Scriptures, Sermons, or else where and also be made able to vse the same aptly themselues.

Set forth by R. C. and newly corrected, and much inlarged with many words now in vse.

Title-page of a pioneer work, Robert Cawdrey's Dictionary of 1604. Much slighter than Johnson's work, it was nevertheless the first English dictionary.

The great Doctor
The most extraordinary literary figure of the age was Dr Samuel Johnson (1709–84). A huge ungainly man, he suffered from scrofula, a skin disease which partly caused his grimaces, strange gestures and mutterings.

At table, he would eat with ravenous greed, belching and snorting like an animal, and his temper, frayed beyond repair by years of humiliating poverty, would explode in fury upon anyone who offended him.

Yet this uncouth character became the centre of a literary circle that included the finest artists and writers of the day. At the coffee house, Johnson's audience listened entranced as he boomed out his views on life and literature. Boswell's *Life of Johnson* became a classic, and his friends loved him because, under that coarse exterior, there dwelt a kind-hearted and intensely lonely man.

Theatre and Music

Georgian drama lacked the vigour and originality of preceding eras. Plays tended to be sentimental and trivial, and even Garrick, the star actor-manager of this age, put on mangled versions of Shakespeare to please middle-class theatre-goers. Dramatists were ill-paid and only Sheridan, Goldsmith and Congreve wrote plays which are still acted today. Nevertheless, theatres were popular, not merely in London, but in Dublin and provincial places like Nottingham, Norwich, Bath and Ipswich, which received regular visits from the leading actors.

As far as music was concerned, Italian opera was in vogue for a time, with rival prima-donnas enjoying notoriety, but its popularity waned and the rough humour of the *Beggar's Opera* was more to the common people's taste. The greatest figure in English music was Handel, a German who settled permanently in the country and received the patronage of both George I and George II, for whom he wrote some of his superb compositions. Thomas Arne, composer of *Rule Britannia*, was the only other musician of note, though there were several writers of popular songs and composers of good church music.

The theatre scene

Though actors and actresses were somewhat better-paid and respected, they suffered from the fact that London's theatres were reduced to only two—Drury Lane and Covent Garden (from 1732)—where straight plays could be produced. Other playhouses led a precarious existence, putting on "irregular" plays with music, dancing and pantomime. In 1737, censorship of plays by the Lord Chamberlain was introduced.

Audiences

A particular nuisance was the custom of allowing privileged spectators to sit on the stage, crowding the actors and hindering the view of other play-goers. Attempts to clear the stage caused riots until, under Garrick's strong management at Drury Lane, the custom was put to an end in 1746.

Another handicap to actors was the behaviour of audiences. Young sparks would stroll about, chat to their friends and ogle the ladies; people hissed and booed the players if anything displeased them, hurled rotten fruit and even rushed the stage to break up scenery, boxes and effects.

Fire risks

Candle-lit theatres, full of draughts, wooden seats and flimsy scenery, were always liable to danger from fire and Garrick's introduction of footlights added another risk to the long dresses of actresses. Covent Garden, twice, and Drury Lane were burned to the ground but they soon rose again from the ashes.

Hogarth's caricature of the *Beggar's Opera*, John Gay's lively, vulgar skit on Italian opera. Its gibes at government brought a ban on similar productions.

David Garrick (1717–79) the great actor, who came to London penniless like his friend Johnson and went on the stage, where his natural style brought him leading roles in London, Dublin and elsewhere. As manager of Drury Lane, he introduced footlights, better scenery and effects.

A theatre at Louis XIV's Court, in the style which influenced English theatre-building. The royal party sits facing an arched stage, the audience at the sides. From this developed the traditional theatre with its proscenium stage set back from the audience who could see better but were less involved in the play.

Keyboard of the organ (left) which Handel gave to a Hospital for Foundling Children in 1750, and (above) part of a fair copy of Handel's *Messiah*.

Music in England

"What the English like is something they can beat time to, something that strikes them straight on the ear", remarked Handel rather sarcastically. Yet their love of simple melodious music accounted for his own popularity and for the rejection of the artificiality of Italian opera.

Singing was still their chief joy and there was a wealth of popular songs, but orchestras were growing out of small groups of musicians (the Duke of Chandos had a private orchestra of 27 players) and instruments like the harpsichord, guitar and viola were heard even in the homes of fox-hunting squires.

George Frederick Handel came to England to make a living from opera but later devoted himself to writing choral music (oratorios), such as *The Messiah*, and compositions like the *Water Music* and *Firework Music* for his royal patrons. This cultured, kindly man, who often gave concerts for charity, became a national favourite; audiences would weep when his most tender arias were sung and George II rose to his feet in admiration of the magnificent *Hallelujah Chorus*.

Travel

In the early part of the century, Britain's roads were in appalling condition; almost nothing had been done to them since Roman times and improvement first came from the turnpike trusts. Companies took over stretches of road and collected tolls to pay for repairs. Unfortunately, little was known about road construction, though General Wade built 250 miles of good roads in Scotland after the "Fifteen".

Traffic flowed more freely as roads improved. Stage-wagons, rumbling along at two or three miles an hour, replaced pack-horses, regular stagecoach services ran between principal towns and Royal Mail Coaches became the crack vehicles on the road. Nevertheless, transport by road remained slow and expensive.

Heavy goods like coal, grain and timber were best moved by water, in barges on the rivers and new canals or by coastal vessels. James Brindley's Worsley Canal (1761) halved the price of coal in Manchester and a network of canals in the Midlands and the North was speedily built to link up with the country's navigable rivers.

Hazards of travel

Apart from the danger of being robbed by highwaymen, travellers had to endure a good deal of discomfort. The stagecoach passenger was jolted and bumped over bad roads (carriage springs were invented in 1704 but they often broke); sometimes the coach got stuck or turned over and he had to walk. If he was an "outside" passenger, riding on the roof, he was frozen in winter and covered with dust in summer; poorer travellers went by stage-wagon, perched among the bales of

A highwayman, said to be Dick Turpin, leaps the turnpike to escape his pursuers.

goods and sleeping in barns at night, but travellers on foot were spurned by everyone.

Costly travel

In the early part of the century, stage-coaches took six days to travel from London to Newcastle (274 miles) and two days to Birmingham (110 miles). By 1785, these times had been halved but it was still expensive to put up at an inn every night, where prices were high and everyone expected a tip.

On turnpike roads, travellers had to pay 1d ($\frac{1}{2}$p) if on horseback and the charge was 6d ($2\frac{1}{2}$p) for a coach and 1s (5p) for a wagon. Since these tolls occurred every ten miles or so, people went out of their way across fields to avoid paying, and dashing riders would sometimes leap clean over a turnpike.

A mail coach: because of lazy, dishonest postboys, mail coaches were introduced. A guard protected the mailbags and passengers helped pay the cost of transport.

Stubbs' picture of the Prince of Wales' phaeton and pair. Private transport was a luxury which only a few could afford and the phaeton was an aristocratic vehicle with high springs at the back from which leather straps supported the body. Light and fast, it normally carried two passengers.

The Advance of Science

During this period, the Royal Society continued to encourage science. All important discoveries and theories were demonstrated and debated by its members, and foreign scientists frequently attended its meetings. Another notable aid to learning was the founding of the British Museum in 1753, for here was assembled an incomparable collection of books, documents and works of art and science.

Astronomers at Greenwich included Edmund Halley, who correctly predicted the sun's eclipse in 1715 and the appearance of Halley's Comet in 1758, and James Bradley who compiled a catalogue of the stars. His calculations also helped to bring the English calendar into line with Continental Gregorian calendar. All the coasts of Britain were surveyed and expeditions went to the south seas to map the stars for navigators.

Men became increasingly curious about the world they lived in. Electricity was the new marvel; "air" was found to contain carbon dioxide and hydrogen; the properties of heat were examined, and these advances in knowledge produced better instruments, machines and industrial processes.

A watch and watch-interior made in about 1700 by Thomas Tompion, greatest of English watch- and clock-makers. His work, highly esteemed on the Continent, included barometers, sun-dials and navigational instruments.

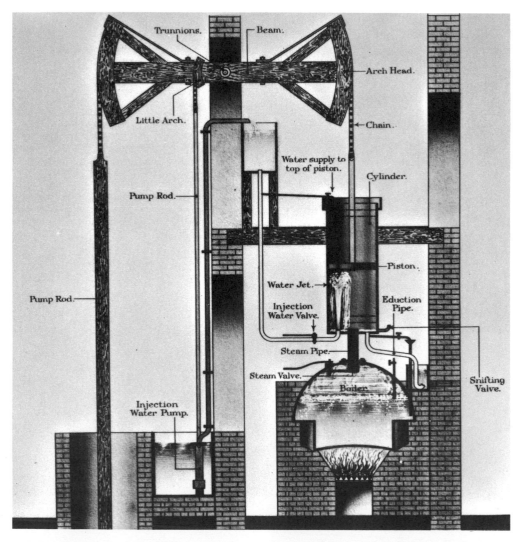

Diagram showing how Newcomen's steam-engine worked. Steam is produced in the boiler and fills the cylinder during the piston's upward stroke.

The steam valve is then closed, a jet of cold water condenses the steam to cause a vacuum under the piston.

Atmospheric pressure on top of the piston forces it down (hence the name "atmospheric" engine).

The piston is raised again by the weight of the pump rod, and this up-and-down movement supplies the pumping action necessary to raise water from the mine below.

In view of the conditions of most schools, it is surprising to find such interest in science. A few public schools were emerging, but many of the grammar schools had fallen into decay and little was taught except Latin.

At the universities, the idleness of students and dons was notorious. However, wealthy parents would provide their sons with tutors to accompany them to school and on the Grand Tour, while Nonconformists had founded a number of Dissenting Academies. At these, boys from middle-class families were taught languages, literature, history and science.

A private school, where the parson teaches Latin and a few rudiments of mathematics and geography.

Discoveries and inventions

Back in 1600, William Gilbert had published his researches into magnetism and had invented the name "electricity". Newton had observed some of the characteristics of electricity but it was Francis Hauksbee who, in 1709, made the first friction machine to produce static electricity.

Stephen Gray worked on conductors and insulators, while William Watson and John Smeaton improved the Dutch Leyden Jar, an early type of electrical condenser. In America, Benjamin Franklin distinguished between positive and negative electricity and invented the lightning conductor.

Better instruments

Progress in astronomy, along with the Navy's requirements, called for better instruments. John Harrison's chronometer enabled sailors to make accurate observations of longitude; the work of John Hadley and Captain Campbell produced the sextant, while various instrument-makers improved the telescope. John Smeaton, bridge and canal-builder, expert on pulleys and the mariner's compass, also rebuilt Eddystone lighthouse in 1759 and did it well enough to last 118 years.

Henry Cavendish, working alone and telling no-one of his findings, discovered hydrogen and made many electrical experiments.

Experiments with steam

As early as 1698, Captain Thomas Savery demonstrated to the Royal Society his engine for raising water "by fire", but it was several years before

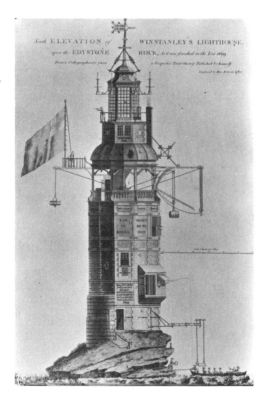

The first Eddystone Lighthouse, a fantastic structure built by Henry Winstanley in 1699, on a dangerous reef some 14 miles from Plymouth. Holes were bored in the rock to hold the base and the light consisted of reflected candle-light. Winstanley perished when his creation was swept away in a great storm of 1703.

Thomas Newcomen produced a more practical steam-engine to pump water out of coal-mines. It did the job clumsily, but one advance led to another and it was Black's work on the properties of steam that later enabled Watt to produce an efficient condenser.

Isaac Newton (1642–1727)

Professor Einstein, the great scientist, said that Newton "determined the course of Western thought, research and practice to an extent that nobody before or since his time can touch". In mathematics, astronomy, physics, chemistry, botany and medicine, Newton made discoveries which have guided generations of scientists.

But he was by no means purely a thinker, since he did practical work on lenses, made a refracting telescope, solved problems that baffled Europe's best mathematicians and, as Master of the Mint, reformed the coinage.

Medicine and Hospitals

Until Queen Anne's reign, there was little or no medical training in Britain, and most doctors were trained abroad in Paris, at Leyden in Holland or at Gottingen in Germany. However, from 1705, medicine began to be taught systematically at Edinburgh and presently at Cambridge, Glasgow and Oxford. Surgeons were looked on as inferior to physicians, yet, because of wars, they probably had better practical knowledge of their art. Moreover, a number of great Scottish surgeons came to the fore, notably Alexander Munro and William and John Hunter, who, with their pupils, made tremendous advances in medical science.

Numbers of new hospitals were founded. In 1714, London had only two, St Bartholomew's and St Thomas's; by 1760, five more general hospitals had been opened, besides three for maternity cases and one for smallpox. The provinces, Ireland and Scotland appear to have had only one hospital before 1714 but by 1760, there were 20. Diseases of soldiers and sailors, in particular, were studied, so that the cause of scurvy came to be understood.

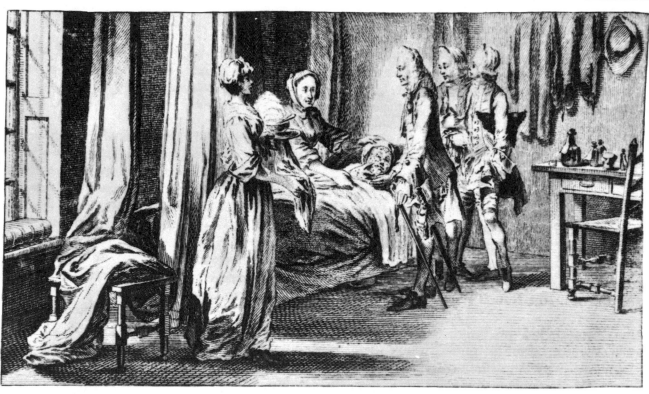

Doctors visit a smallpox victim. The disease was widespread and highly contagious; patients died or were left scarred and pitted for life.

Treatment for disease

Lady Mary Wortley Montagu, a celebrated traveller, came back from Constantinople in 1718 with an account of how the Turks inoculated themselves with a small amount of smallpox "matter" and thus avoided serious attacks of the disease.

Smallpox was so rife at this time that a great many persons, including the Royal Family, underwent Lady Mary's "cure". In fact, it did little or nothing to wipe out the dreaded illness, which was not controlled until vaccination came in at the end of the century.

People still believed in semi-magical remedies and ghastly brews like snail tea, but observation and experiment were beginning to produce results. James Lind, for instance, recommended fresh fruit and lime juice to avoid scurvy and John Pringle showed that wounds could be treated with antiseptics.

People were also beginning to understand the connection between disease and bad sanitation.

Picture of a chemist's laboratory; its size and the number of assistants speak for the importance of apothecaries, who resembled present-day General Practitioners. They treated patients and prescribed medicines, calling in the physician for serious cases. As they were not allowed to charge for treatment, they put the price on their medicines.

18th Century doctors

Surgeons broke away from the barbers in 1745 to form their own Company and, from then on, their training, knowledge and reputation vastly improved.

There were three kinds of physicians: (i) members of the Royal College of Physicians, an exclusive group of wealthy practitioners (only 52 of them in 1745); (ii) Licentiates of the College, also few in number and usually better trained; (iii) Apothecaries who mixed medicines and treated many more patients than the others.

In addition, there were hundreds of quacks and frauds who provided outrageous remedies for those who paid their fees.

A ward in Guy's Hospital in 1725, the year when it was opened. Thomas Guy, who made a fortune before the South Sea Bubble burst, built the hospital and left over £200,000 for its upkeep.

Bethleham Hospital or Bedlam, the first lunatic asylum in England. Inmates were brutally ill-treated and put on show to amuse the public.

Women's ward in the Middlesex Hospital, another of the new hospitals of this period. Admission was free, though you had to have influence to get in; operations, conducted without drugs, except brandy, were becoming more skilled and midwifery was studied scientifically, instead of being left to ignorant old women.

King and Colonists

The breach between Britain and her American colonies was inevitable. The colonists now included a vast number who had no connection with the Mother Country and no feeling of loyalty towards the Crown. Quite naturally, they wanted to be free from restraints imposed from a country 3,000 miles away. These restraints were far from petty. Britain looked to the colonies to supply raw materials and to buy manufactured goods on terms which kept the colonial merchants permanently in debt. Nor, in law, could the colonies do business with anyone else, and, on top of these commercial disadvantages, were the perpetual squabbles between British officials and colonial assemblies who wanted to manage their own affairs.

In George III's view, however, the colonists were disobedient subjects who wrong-headedly refused to pay their share of the cost of the recent war. The British had saved them from French domination, and the vast new territories had to be guarded. Therefore, colonists, whether they liked it or not, must be taxed. On this issue, the colonists took up arms.

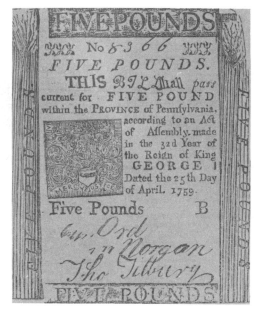

An American banknote issued in 1759. The colonies had no mint or regular currency and banknotes were often worth less than their face value, a great hindrance to trade.

Anti-English feelings

After the French had been defeated, certain radical groups of colonists became increasingly anti-British. More moderate people merely wanted their grievances put right.

New settlers constantly arrived from Germany, Holland, Sweden and the Huguenot districts of France, but English immigrants were becoming fewer. Large numbers of Scots and Irish came because they had been denied justice and a decent living at home. Thus, while some were indifferent to England, many others hated her.

George III, aged 22, in his coronation robes. Unlike his father and grandfather, he had been born in England and carefully educated there. He felt himself an Englishman and he responded readily to his mother's advice, "George, be King."

This virtuous, conscientious young man possessed a good capacity for hard work, but in his stubborn determination to put down the "rebellious disposition" of his subjects in America, he failed to understand their refusal to accept what they thought was tyranny. His personal influence was so strong that he has to take a major share of the blame for the war that broke out in 1775.

Young George Washington

Brought up in Virginia, young Washington became a public surveyor of lands along the frontier. He therefore knew the area well and, in 1754, was given command of two companies to expel the French. He began well but was forced to surrender at Fort Necessity.

However, he later fought bravely under Braddock and, after miraculous escapes from death, commanded the border forces and led the vanguard when Forbes captured Fort Duquesne. After the fighting ended, Washington settled down to the life of a rich planter on his estate on Mount Vernon.

George Washington (1732–99) as a young army officer.

General Edward Braddock who was sent out to Virginia with two regiments in 1755. Taking Washington on his staff, he advanced on Fort Duquesne, but his force was cut to pieces by French and Indians firing from cover. Braddock himself died bravely.

William Shirley (above), Governor of Massachusetts, an enemy of the French in N. America; he took command of the British forces on Braddock's death.

An embroidered quilt (left) showing a colonial scene. The church was the centre of community life and a meeting-place where grievances were aired.

Colonial government

Instead of the colonial assemblies and the British officials working together in harmony, they engaged in a constant tug-of-war.

Some of the officials appointed by the Crown were arrogant and incompetent; few had much sympathy with the colonial point of view. So, there were irritations on both sides. Assemblies would hold back governors' pay and even an able governor like William Shirley never succeeded in getting his regular salary.

Militia officers like Colonel Washington were aggrieved that their rank was not equal to a British officer's.

British Isles and Ireland

A period bursting with achievement in battle, in the arts, science and industry. England and Scotland became united and a Protestant constitutional monarchy put an end to Jacobite hopes. A long series of wars with France resulted in Britain acquiring a world-wide Empire. The giants of this age included Newton, Marlborough, Walpole, Pitt, Wolfe, Clive, Swift, Handel, Wesley, Johnson and Hogarth.

Europe

France, forever at war, was almost always unsuccessful; Sweden knew brief spell of glory; the rise of Frederick the Great's Prussia alarmed everyone; Russia began to emerge from isolation.

	British Isles and Ireland	Europe
1689	The Glorious Revolution: accession of William and Mary; Declaration of Rights. James II defeated in Ireland: siege of Londonderry; Battle of the Boyne; Treaty of Limerick. Jacobite rising in Scotland: Bonnie Dundee killed at Killiecrankie; Massacre of Glencoe (1692). War with France: naval defeat off Beachy Head (1690); French invasion plan thwarted by victory of La Hogue; Anglo-Dutch command at sea. Whig support for William; beginning of National Debt and Stock Exchange; Bank of England founded (1694). Treaty of Ryswick (1697) ended war.	War of the League of Augsburg between Louis XIV's France and a Grand Alliance led by William III. Holand was saved; Treaty of Ryswick (1697) ended war. Charles II of Spain left empire to Louis' grandson, Philip of Anjou. Hungary freed from the Turks. Charles XII, a military genius, became King of Sweden, at war with Poland.
1700	Writers: Locke, Dryden, Congreve. Opera: Purcell. Science: Newton.	Peter the Great began to modernise Russia.
	Act of Settlement established Protestant succession. Death of James II and French recognition of James Edward, the Old Pretender. Accession of Queen Anne. War of Spanish Succession: Rooke captured Gibraltar (1704), defeated French navy at Malaga. Marlborough won Battles of Blenheim (1704), and Ramillies (1706). Act of Union (1707) united England and Scotland to form Great Britain. Old Pretender failed in attempt to invade Scotland. Allied victories at Oudenarde (1708), Malplaquet (1709). Marlborough dismissed due to Whig decline and loss of Anne's favour. Tory government elected. Peace with France at Treaty of Utrecht (1713). Bolingbroke harassed Dissenters (Schism Act) and planned to bring over James Edward. Death of Queen Anne; accession of George I (1714); Whigs back in power. The "Fifteen", Jacobite rising in Scotland; Battle of Sheriffmuir, James Edward returned to France. Septennial Act (1716) extended parliaments to seven years. Triple Alliance (Britain, France, Holland) and Quadruple Alliance (those plus Austria) made war on Spain: Byng's victory at Cape Passaro. "South Sea Bubble" (1720); financial panic; Robert Walpole became Chancellor of the Exchequer and, in effect, the first Prime Minister. First daily newspaper in England. *Gulliver's Travels* published. Augustan Age of literature: Swift, Steele, Pope, Addison, Defoe; Music: Handel.	War of Spanish Succession: France and Spain against alliance headed by England, Austria and Holland. France defeated and brought to verge of ruin. Treaties of Utrecht and Baden ended war: Philip V confirmed King of Spain; Austria gained Spanish Netherlands. Charles of Austria became Emperor. Louis XIV died (1715), Regent Orléans friendly with England. Great Northern War: Charles XII fought brilliantly against Denmark, Poland, Russia; killed in 1718. In France, Mississippi Company boomed and collapsed. Russo-Turkish war: Austria defeated Turks at Belgrade (1717). Charles VI's Pragmatic Sanction settled Habsburg succession on Maria Theresa. Cristofori of Florence made first piano. J S Bach composed great music in Germany, and Scarlatti in Italy. Gabriel D Fahrenheit devised mercury thermometer. Voltaire writing in France.
1725	Science: Halley; Newcomen's steam-engine.	
	Accession of George II (1727); Queen Caroline kept Walpole in power. Treaty of Seville (1729) ended war with Spain. John and Charles Wesley founded Methodist Society. *Beggar's Opera* performed. Walpole forced to drop his Excise Bill (1733). Porteous Riots (1736) in Edinburgh. Growth of opposition to Walpole's one-man rule. War of Jenkin's Ear (1739) with Spain developed into War of Austrian Succession against France. Portobello captured; defeat at Carthagena; Anson's voyage. Walpole resigned (1641), succeeded by Pelham and Cartaret. George II fought at Dettingen (1743); Cumberland defeated at Fontenoy (1745). The "Forty-five", last Jacobite rising; Charles Edward invaded England, but defeated by Cumberland at Culloden. Highlands subjugated. Treaty of Aix-la-Chapelle (1748) ended the war. Literary and artistic age: freedom of Press established. Satires of Swift, Pope, Arbuthnot; rise of the novel—Fielding, Defoe, Smollett, Richardson; essays of Hume, Johnson; poetry of Gray and Collins. Music: Handel and Thomas Arne. Architecture: the Adams brothers. Art: Hogarth. Acting: Garrick. Science: Stephen Hales, botanist; James Bradley, astronomer; Stephen Gray, electrical pioneer; James Hadley invented sextant; John Harrison, first chronometer. Agriculture: "Turnip" Townshend and Bakewell.	War between England and Spain; ended by Treaty of Seville (1729). Fleury, chief minister 1726–43, brought recovery to France. War of Polish Succession (1733–35); France, Spain and Sardinia against Russia and Austria, who won and put their candidate on the throne. But in Italy, France and Spain beat Austria; Naples and Sicily became Spanish possessions. Austro-Russian alliance defeated Turkey. Maria Theresa became Empress of Austria (1740). Frederick II of Prussia seized Silesia; hence war of Austrian Succession, with Prussia, France, Bavaria, Saxony and Spain versus Austria, Britain, Hanover (and, later, Russia and Poland); ended by Treaty of Aix-la-Chapelle (1747); nothing decided. Russia, under Elizabeth (1741–62), developed learning. In Italy, paintings of Canaletto, Tiepolo. In France, writings of Voltaire, Prévost, Diderot. In Sweden, Linnaeus, the great botanist.
1750	Industry: Kay's Flying Shuttle (1733), cotton manufacture.	
	Britain adopted the Gregorian Calendar (1752). Newcastle in power, rise of William Pitt. Anglo-French hostilities in North America and India. Seven Years' War began (1756) in alliance with Prussia; Admiral Byng executed for loss of Minorca. Pitt took control. British success at sea, in Canada and India. Year of Victories 1759. Accession of George III (1760); resignation of Pitt and end of war by Treaty of Paris (1763). Joseph Black identified carbon dioxide. British Museum opened.	Seven Years' (or Third Silesian) War 1756–63; Britain and Prussia against France, Austria, Russia, Sweden, Denmark and Spain. Frederick the Great, with British subsidies and some troops, won brilliant victories (e.g. Rossbach, Leuthen, Zorndorf, Liegnitz) but was about to be overwhelmed by Russia when saved by Elizabeth's death. War ended by Treaties of Paris and Hubertsburg. Frederick felt he had been deserted. In France, Rousseau's writings.
1763	Gainsborough's paintings. Smeaton's lighthouse. Bradley's star catalogue.	

Asia

China, expansionist under two great emperors, kept Europeans at arm's length, but, in India, the break-up of Mogul power enabled the British to increase their commercial and political hold.

Peter the Great began modernizing Russia; made treaty with China; attacked Turkey; took Azov.
Mogul Empire in India declined under Aurangzeb, though literature, painting and architecture still flourished. In Bengal, British founded Calcutta (1690). Anglo-French rivalry.
Manchu or Ch'ing Dynasty in China: K'ang Hsi (1661–1722) expanded empire, captured Formosa, allowed European traders only at Macao, near Canton.

Afghanistan won independence from Persia.
Russians, Turks and Afghans attacked Persia.
India: death of Aurangzeb led to civil war among princes.
Deccan became virtually independent of Mogul rule; Sikhs emerged as strongly militant order.
English East India Company gained trade concessions.
Tokugama (or Edo) period in Japan; rapid growth of Edo (Tokyo) and merchant class.
Country ruled by a *shogun* (military dictator), prime minister and bureaucratic class. Revival of learning, with novels, poetry, drama, puppetry and wood-block art. Foreigners mostly excluded and less Chinese influence. Religion a mixture of Confucianism, *bushido* (feudal code of conduct) and Shintoism.
Chinese successfully invaded Tibet (1720).

Russia continued to expand; Turkish Empire in decline.
Brief rise of Persia: Nadir, a tribal chief, defeated Afghans and Turks, made himself Shah, invaded India and captured Delhi (1739).
In India, power of Grand Mogul further declined; rise of the Mahrattas. French, under Dupleix, made much progress in Deccan and Carnatic; captured Madras from British.
Ch'ien Lung (1736–96), grandson of K'ang Hsi, made war on Nepal, Burma, Annam. A cultured ruler who tolerated Jesuits in return for medical, scientific and map-making services, but attempts to fuse Christian and Chinese beliefs failed when the Pope condemned Chinese religious practice (1742). Europeans excluded, apart from some limited trading.

Dutch dominated East Indies from Malacca, centre of spice trade.
Clive's defence of Arcot (1751) and capture of Trichinopoly restored British position in India.
Surajah Dowlah seized Calcutta but defeated by Clive at Plassey.
Mir Jaffa installed as Nawab of Bengal under British protection. French ousted and their East India Company dissolved.

Africa

North Africa freed itself from Turkish rule; European powers acquired trading-stations on the coasts. The slave trade intensified, but Africa's interior remained almost unknown to Europeans.

French conquered Senegal.
Decline of Turkish power in North Africa; Tunis and Algiers grew rich on piracy.
Growth of Moroccan power under Ismail.
Iyasu the Great in Abyssinia prevented inroads of Islam and European powers.
Portuguese expelled from East Coast, except Mozambique.
Gradual destruction of Negro cultures, due to Western influence and the slave trade.

Decline of Ottoman Empire allowed N. African states to break free. Morocco virtually independent under Sultan Mulay Ismail: Europeans expelled. Husein ben Ali founded dynasty in Tunisia.
European navies reduced activities of the Algerian *corsairs* (pirates).
France and Spain obtained trading-posts.
Decline of Songhoi Empire in the Sudan.
Anarchy in Abyssinia; massacre of Catholics (1719).
Slave trade at its height in West Africa: by the *asiento*, Spain granted England the right to supply slaves to Spanish American colonies.
French took Mauritius (1715).
English conquered Gambia (1723).

Anarchy in Morocco after death of Ismail.
Spread of Islam across Negro Africa.
Revival of Swahili culture in East Africa.
Rule of Beys in Egypt: trade and commerce languished.

Sultan Malay Mehemet drove Portuguese from Morocco; made trade agreements with Europeans, granted monopoly to Danes in Atlantic; advantages to French and Dutch in the Mediterranean.
British captured French possessions in Senegal (1758).
Dutch in South Africa expanded northwards and crossed Orange River.

The Americas

Britain and Spain emerged as the dominant colonial powers in the American world, but the colonists of North America were beginning to feel a sense of unity and a desire for self-rule.

The French began to colonise Louisiana.
Hostilities between French and English colonists but Treaty of Ryswick restored conquests.
Massachusetts absorbed Plymouth colony.
Spain recaptured New Mexico.
Earthquake in Jamaica and foundation of Kingston.
Portuguese expanded in Brazil and discovered gold: Spaniards increased hold on Peru and Venezuela.

During Spanish Succession War, hostility between French and English in North America, and between Spanish, Portuguese and French in South America.
By Treaty of Utrecht (1713), Britain gained *asiento* to sell slaves to Spanish colonies; also gained Newfoundland, Nova Scotia (Acadia) and Hudson's Bay country.
Detroit, founded (1701). German immigration in Pennsylvania, French settled Alabama. Indian wars in Carolina: separation of North and South Carolina.
Spain took Texas, as result of war with France.
Governor Burnet of New York made treaties with Indians to counter French influence in the West.

During War of Jenkin's Ear, Spain generally held on to her possessions. By Treaty of Madrid (1750) recognised Portuguese claims in South America. Britain gave up *asiento* (1750).
James Oglethorne founded Georgia, 13th and last British colony.
Benjamin Franklin published *Poor Richard's Almanac*.

French seized Ohio valley, defeated Virginian troops under Washington, ambushed Braddock's force at Fort Duquesne (1755). Franklin's plan for a union of colonies rejected by Albany Convention.
Wolfe captured Quebec (1759). By Treaty of Paris France lost Canada and all possessions east of Mississippi. Spain ceded Florida to Britain. Rising of Indian tribes against the British who had taken over French forts.

Index

Europe c.1740

ATLANTIC OCEAN

SWEDISH EMPIRE

Finland

SCOTLAND

①

IRELAND

②

DENMARK and NORWAY

NORTH SEA

RUSSIA

BALTIC SEA

③

WALES

ENGLAND

④

⑤

Prussia

UNITED PROVINCES

Hanover

PRUSSIA

POLAND

ENGLISH CHANNEL

⑦

Austrian Netherlands

Palatinate

Saxony

Silesia

⑥

THE EMPIRE

Bohemia

FRANCE

Bavaria

Austria

⑧

HUNGARY

SWITZERLAND

SAVOY

VENICE

⑨

⑩

⑪

OTTOMAN EMPIRE

SPAIN

Corsica

Minorca

Sardinia

PAPAL STATES

⑫

SICILY

MEDITERRANEAN SEA